TWO
ROADS

Dear Reader

Since I published *Marley & Me* over five years ago, I feel I've seen hundreds of animal memoirs. Marley certainly started a trend. But books have to lead, not follow, and since that time, I have published only a select few that I believe are saying something different. Animal stories are, of course, as much about the humans as about the animals, and *The Puppy Diaries* is as much about a woman at a certain point in her life as about an adorable puppy.

Jill Abramson, as Executive Editor of the *New York Times*, respected journalist, empty nester and dog-lover, brings a certain New York sensibility to this account of a dog's first year. Part memoir, part investigative report (she is a journalist after all), this book has been pitched in-house as Nora Ephron meets *Marley & Me*. I've loved this from the very first line: 'The truth about getting a new dog is that it makes you miss the old one.' Hope you do too.

Lisa Highton
PUBLISHER

the Puppy Diaries

the
Puppy
Diaries

raising a dog named Scout

JILL ABRAMSON

www.tworoadsbooks.com

First published in Great Britain in 2011 by
Two Roads
An imprint of Hodder & Stoughton
An Hachette UK company

1

A CIP catalogue record for this title is available from the British Library.

Hardback ISBN 978 1 444 72061 7
Trade Paperback ISBN 978 1 444 72062 4
eBook ISBN 978 1 444 72064 8

Printed and bound in Great Britain by CPI Group (UK), Croydon, CR0 4YY

Hodder & Stoughton policy is to use papers that are natural, renewable
and recyclable products and made from wood grown in sustainable
forests. The logging and manufacturing processes are expected to
conform to the environmental regulations of the country of origin.

Two Roads
Hodder & Stoughton Ltd
338 Euston Road
London NW1 3BH

To Henry

CONTENTS

the
Puppy
Diaries

CHAPTER ONE

The truth about getting a new dog is that it makes you miss the old one.

This reality hit me hard one spring day in 2009 when we arrived at Thistledown Golden Retrievers, near Boston, where my husband, Henry, and I had come to meet Donna Cutler, a breeder of English golden retrievers. Because it was named Thistledown, and because I knew that the golden retriever breed was started by someone actually named Lord Tweedmouth, I was expecting the place to look like a country manor.

Instead, we parked in front of a plain suburban ranch, and the only hint of the litter of the seven-

week-old puppies we had been invited to inspect—
though we knew it was really us who had to pass
muster with the breeder—was a sign on the front
door that showed two golden retrievers and said WIPE
YOUR PAWS. Why did I suddenly feel like wiping my
eyes?

My heart was still hurting over the loss of Buddy,
our stone-deaf, feisty-to-the-end West Highland white
terrier, who had died in March 2007 at age fourteen.
Our two children, Cornelia and Will, who grew up
with him but flew the nest years before his demise,
often mused that Buddy was my one perfect relationship in life.

Buddy, like me, was a self-sufficient type, and
despite his small size he was no lap dog. Like many
Westies, he was woefully stubborn and never once
came when called. He could be unpredictable and
grouchy around small children and once bit my god-
daughter's upper lip. He wasn't great with old people,
either; years later, he bit the leg of an elderly woman
who, for some inexplicable reason, was standing bare-
foot and dressed in her nightgown in our elevator when
the doors opened on our floor. (Happily, that incident triggered an unlikely friendship between Eve,
Buddy's victim, and me.) Nonetheless, I was madly in
love and forgave Buddy all his sins. I learned a lot from
him, too; among other things, he taught me that

Buddy and Jill on the porch in Connecticut

even in stressful situations dogs have a unique way of steering you in unlikely and interesting directions.

I confess that I spoiled Buddy beyond all reason. Houseguests often awoke to the aroma of grilled chicken with a dusting of rosemary, which I liked to give him for breakfast. Henry would sometimes note, without rancor, that when I took business trips and called home, my first question was always "How's Buddy?"

Long after Cornelia and Will began to wriggle out of my embraces and find my made-up games annoying, Buddy was always happy to have me scratch his pink belly and play tug-of-war. While my children filled their lives with school, scouting, and sports—and, later, college, work, and love—Buddy remained my steadfast companion.

When Buddy was a puppy, we lived in Virginia, and together he and I would amble around our neighborhood for miles, discovering new side streets with interesting houses. Someone always stopped to admire him, which is how I met a lot of my neighbors. During our walks I was also able to let go of some of the pressure of my job as an investigative reporter, back then for the *Wall Street Journal*. Sometimes, with my mind wandering free as I pulled the leash this way and that, I would come up with a great story idea or reporting angle on the Washington scandals that were my frequent report-ing targets. Buddy, steadfast and true, was my loyal coconspirator.

I once experienced a rare eureka moment while on a walk with Buddy. I had recently left the *Journal* and gone to work in the Washington bureau of the *New York Times*, where I was on the team of reporters covering the Monica Lewinsky scandal. One day in late 1998, as Buddy and I strolled up Second Street South in Arlington, I realized that one of the people I had encountered in a document the previous night was familiar to me; he was a prominent conservative lawyer in New York. Why his name surfaced in my brain during a walk with Buddy the next morning is anyone's guess, but when Buddy and I got home, I took out the documents I had been reviewing and found that this lawyer was mentioned repeatedly. That dis-covery led to a front-page story about how a cabal of conservative lawyers had secretly worked on the sexual harassment case that triggered impeachment proceed-ings against President Bill Clinton. Buddy, my silent partner, deserved to share the byline on that story.

Although independent and often fierce, Buddy was always happy to see me. When my children were in their late teens, I couldn't help but notice that he, unlike Cornelia and Will, was never sullen and didn't ask to borrow the car. And when I became the *Times's* Washington bureau chief, I noted that unlike the reporters who worked for me, Buddy was unfailingly delighted whenever I came up with what I thought was an inspired idea.

Buddy, you see, was my first dog, and I had fallen hard. Perhaps this new relationship was so intense partly because it wasn't based on words, unlike the rest of my personal and professional life. I spent so much of my day talking, reading, and writing that it was both a relief and a joy to spend time with Buddy. Except for a few simple commands, our conversation consisted entirely of my silly cooings and his appreciative grunts.

My older sister, Jane, has often observed that what she found most surprising about me was my late-in-life transformation into a dog lover. "You were a wonderful parent," she once told me, "but I've never seen you so affectionate or expressive with anyone the way you are with this dog." It was true. At work, where some of my colleagues and sources said they found my tough-girl investigative journalist persona intimidating, I was constantly pulling out the latest snapshots of Buddy and telling everyone my latest dog stories. Buddy was more than my coconspirator; he also seemed to certify me as a nicer person.

It wasn't just Buddy. I also adored Arrow, my sister's Jack Russell mix, who greeted me with ecstasy at her door. Arrow and I formed a special bond when I moved from Washington to New York in 2003 to become the *Times*'s managing editor. Henry—who worked at a Washington, D.C., think tank and was in the process of becoming a consultant in New York—and Buddy weren't able to join me in Manhattan right away, so I lived for a couple of weeks with Jane; her husband, Jim; and Arrow. My love affair with Arrow was kindled during this period by the doggy bags I often brought home from the swanky restaurants where I had business dinners. Arrow, I recall, was especially fond of the grilled liver and bacon from an Italian place called Elio's.

I grew up in an apartment on Manhattan's Upper West Side. Our parents allowed Jane and me to have turtles, fish, parakeets, and even a hamster, who outlived all our other pets. (During the famous blackout of 1965, I spent hours funneling water into a tropical fish tank to provide enough oxygen to save a pregnant fantail guppy and her impending brood.) But my parents drew the line at a dog. "The city is not a good place to raise a puppy," my mother told us. Despite our pleas, and even though we lived across from Central Park, she was unyielding.

Buddy arrived in 1992, when Henry and I were in our late thirties and our kids were nine and seven. That was also the year my father died, so Buddy was especially welcome. Cornelia and Will told the usual children's fib about getting a pet: they assured me that they would faithfully feed and walk this adorable addition to our family. It didn't work out that way, of course, so I took care of Buddy, training him, feeding him, and singing him to sleep in his tiny crate. I didn't mind, though; having new life in our house was a tonic for my grief over the loss of my dad.

Our setup in those days was perfect for an active puppy. We lived in an unfashionable corner of Arlington, Virginia, in a sturdy bungalow ordered out of the 1928 Sears catalog. The house came with a large fenced yard, and since Buddy had a little dog door he could come and go as he pleased. His purpose in life became patrolling our patch of lawn and protecting us from a host of imagined intruders. He also learned to open our mail slot; every day, he would wait inside for the mailman to arrive and then race onto our porch to retrieve the day's post. When it snowed, Buddy would often disappear under the white mounds in our yard and then tunnel and burrow to his heart's content. I especially loved to walk him when the snow was crunchy under my boots—amazingly, Buddy made me look forward to winter.

Buddy was already eleven when we arrived in Manhattan, and I worried that the move might kill him. We sublet a loft downtown, in Tribeca, but happily Buddy loved all the action in his new neighborhood, including the smells of so many other dogs and the fishy sidewalk outside a high-end Japanese restaurant called Nobu.

Once Henry and I settled into our own place in the same neighborhood, I hired a dog walker named Carlos, who took Buddy for a walk each afternoon. Once, when I forgot to bring some papers to work, I returned home to retrieve them and bumped into Carlos on the street walking Buddy in a pack with three other dogs. Buddy hadn't socialized much with other dogs during his yard-patrolling years, but now he seemed perfectly at ease with his cool city friends. When he saw me that day, he regarded me with a dismissive "What are you doing here?" look.

Before going to work, I often took Buddy to a dog run near the Hudson River where he bonded with a Scottie about his size. They looked like an advertisement for scotch when they romped together, and I enjoyed chatting with the other owners, who sat on benches and loved arguing with me about the theater, movie, and dining reviews in the *Times*. These mornings reminded me of the years when my kids were toddlers and I made a number of good friends while sitting on benches in the playground, talking about everything from biodegradable diapers to our marriages.

One day when I took Buddy for a checkup to the veterinarian in Tribeca, I encountered a woman with two Westies. The woman was wearing a pair of plaid socks emblazoned with Westies. "I have the same pair," I told her. She laughed and then looked at Buddy. "How old is your Westie?" she asked. When I told her Buddy was thirteen, she said, "Oh, we have an eighteen-year-old." Since the two dogs accompanying her were obviously much younger, I asked where the older one was. "He lives in a hospice nearby, and we visit him almost every day," she replied. I was stunned, never having imagined the existence of live-in, end-of-life care for dogs. This encounter marked the beginning of my fascination with the rarefied world of Manhattan dog owners, some of whom seek out dog hospices—not to mention dog massage therapists and dog shrinks who dispense antianxiety medications.

Henry and I were also startled to discover that everything having to do with dogs is so much more expensive in Manhattan than in Arlington. Although we live in an old, unrenovated building that used to be a spice warehouse and has no doorman, Tribeca is one of Manhattan's most expensive neighborhoods, full of Wall Street brokers who earn fat salaries and big bonuses. Signs reading LUXURY LOFTS FOR SALE are everywhere, with *luxury* being code for apartments that sell for two million dollars or more. A rubber ball I purchased at the local "pet boutique" cost six dollars. True, I splurged on a dog walker, but other dog owners in our neighborhood spent even more to send their pups to the Wagging Tail, a doggy day-care center on Greenwich Street.

By the time Buddy turned fourteen, he had lost his hearing, but he was still a hardy boy. In the winter of 2007, though, he developed a persistent cough. "I think it may be his heart," said Cornelia, who was then in her second year of medical school at Columbia. One weekend, he had what seemed like a small stroke: he was temporarily confused but snapped back to his old self pretty quickly. Then, in late February, while Cornelia and I were walking him one evening, he collapsed on the sidewalk. I carried him as we raced to the vet, who told us to take him to an animal hospital on lower Fifth Avenue. After he was given some oxygen, he seemed to stabilize. We were advised to leave him overnight, and I became tearful when we were ushered in to say good night and I saw him lying in a little cage, looking so vulnerable.

At 3 a.m. the telephone rang. It was the vet: Buddy was in full congestive heart failure. "He's having a terrible time breathing and he seems to be in pain," the on-duty vet reported. "I think we should put him down." Cornelia grabbed the phone and said we would be there in just a few minutes.

Henry, Cornelia, and I dashed out of our apartment, almost forgetting our coats in our hurry, and hailed a cab. When we arrived at the animal hospital, Buddy was lying on his side on a gurney, his back heaving up and down, a tiny oxygen mask on his face. We asked a barrage of questions and tried our best to convince ourselves that Buddy could recover, but it was clear there was no hope. As the medical technician prepared the lethal injection, Henry and I couldn't bear to watch, despite the counsel of friends who said that it was comforting to be present when a dog's life came to a peaceful end. Cornelia, in doctor mode, stayed with Buddy to the last.

When we returned to our loft, I felt the silence envelope me. It was heartbreaking; I had become so accustomed to hearing Buddy's metal tags jangle as he walked from room to room. To my ear, that was the music of loyal companionship.

After Buddy died, I was disconsolate. It wasn't simply that I missed the unconditional love or the ecstatic greeting each time I walked in the door, even if I'd been gone for only a few minutes to take the garbage to the basement. I missed everything about our routine, from feeding him grilled chicken to our late-night strolls along the windy riverside. And I assiduously avoided walks that took me anywhere near the dog run.

Most people pushed Henry and me to get another dog right away. But as the weeks passed, I grew accustomed to some aspects of a dogless life. With no dog to walk, I could not only catch up on whatever I hadn't read the previous day in the *Times*, but also scan the *Wall Street Journal*, the *Financial Times*, and a number of Web sites and political blogs—all before work. I got an iPhone and quickly became a master of distracted living, a lifestyle not well suited to the focused playing and training a puppy needs. I filled my digital nest with Facebook friends, including rediscovered distant relatives and former high school classmates. Henry and I often spent weekends in the Connecticut town where he grew up—we had purchased an old farmhouse there in the late 1990s—and now we could go to the beach all day or stay out late without worrying about getting home to let the dog out.

Before long, I had almost convinced myself that my mother was right: the city is probably a bad place for a pup, even one that can live part-time in the country. My days as a dog owner seemed to be over.

Two months after Buddy died, life took another terrible turn. On the morning of May 7, 2007, while walking from my office to a nearby gym, I was struck by a large white truck at West Forty-fourth Street and Seventh Avenue in Times Square. Having grown up in the city, I considered myself an expert navigator of Manhattan's busy streets. Like most New Yorkers, I had had a couple of alarming experiences when a taxi almost clipped me as I stood on a corner or a bicycle messenger whizzed by so close that he touched my jacket. But I walked everywhere in the city and never gave its hazards a second thought.

Now, as I was crossing Seventh Avenue, a huge refrigerated truck making a right turn came barreling straight at me. The truck's right front wheel smashed my right foot and I was dragged to the ground. The truck's rear wheel rolled over my left thigh and snapped the femur. Luckily, other pedestrians stopped to help me. As I lay bleeding in the street, I was conscious but in terrible pain. While some passersby got a policeman to call an ambulance, others chased down and stopped the truck. When the ambulance arrived, paramedics told me I would be taken to Bellevue Hospital, the city's famous trauma center.

I spent the next three weeks in the hospital. Besides my leg and foot injuries, I had broken my pelvis and sustained significant internal injuries. One of the doctors told me that if the truck's rear wheel had struck my left thigh just two inches higher, I would have been killed. After surgeons operated on my leg and inserted a titanium rod, I was told that I would have to spend six weeks in bed and then learn to walk again.

As I began my recovery in Bellevue, I learned to move from bed to wheelchair by using only my arms and upper body. Soon I started an intensive course of physical therapy; working side by side with patients who had sustained terrible head injuries, I realized how lucky I was. The nurses on the front lines of my care were always adroit and warm. I remember that the first time I had to move from my bed to a wheel-chair, my nurse Angela told me to clasp my arms tightly around her neck as she carried my entire weight. "Dance with me, baby," she joked, as she supported my limp body.

Once home, a skilled physical therapist named Pearl visited me three times a week. I was like a baby again, but Pearl taught me how to progress from crawling to walking, first by using crutches and then, finally, a cane. Feeling so helpless was very hard for me, and I became easily frustrated when I couldn't do simple tasks, such as putting clean dishes away in the kitchen.

I missed Buddy terribly during this difficult time— it would have been such a comfort to have him by my side. The climb to get back on my feet was hard, and three months after the accident I still walked unsteadily. But the human body, even in middle age, is remarkably resilient, and my years of dog walking and gym workouts helped the bone grow back over the rod in my leg relatively quickly. Slowly, my physical mobility returned.

Just as I was returning to something approximating normal, a depression descended and seemed to smother me like a hot blanket. I had never experienced anything like it and was somewhat reassured when I learned that an episode of depression is fairly common after a traumatic injury. Fortunately, I was able to get some good counseling from a therapist. During one session, my therapist told me that when I talked about Buddy my whole face lit up. "Maybe you should think about getting another dog," she gently suggested.

Henry, the kids, and Jane Mayer—my best friend and fellow dog nut—promptly launched a massive cheer-up campaign. Their collective diagnosis was a severe case of midlife blues: in the past few years I had turned fifty, seen my grown-up children leave our nest, and lost my beloved Buddy. Now, as I struggled to recover from the accident and my depression, they were certain that what I needed above all else was a new dog.

Over the years, Jane and I had enjoyed many capers, both professional and personal. We had co-written a best-selling book about Supreme Court justice Clarence Thomas, a project that involved some of the most challenging reporting of our careers. This undertaking did have its lighter moments, however; in one instance, our investigation required that we watch X-rated videos featuring a porn star named Bad Mama Jama, and they were so ridiculous and boring that we both fell asleep on my living room couch. A couple of years earlier, we had rescued Jane's lovable yellow Lab, Peaches, from the clutches of a very bad boyfriend who had insisted on keeping Peaches after he and Jane split up. One hot Friday, as I was planning a drive to New England for a summer vacation with the kids and Buddy, Jane enlisted my help in a plot to kidnap Peaches. That afternoon, while the boyfriend was still at work, we pulled up to his house in my creaky green minivan. Jane was so tiny that she had no trouble sneaking into the house through the dog door. In a flash, she emerged through the front door with Peaches, who clambered into the minivan next to Buddy as I stepped on the gas and we sped away.

Now, as part of a relentless campaign to lift my spirits, Jane sent me pictures of a pair of elderly basset hound sisters who needed a home. She suggested that we each take one, but I put her off, arguing that these good old girls should not be torn asunder. Cornelia weighed in by announcing that we should think about names for a new dog, and she regularly e-mailed me with ideas such as Cosmo, Sugar, and Pamplona. Will, not to be outdone, sent me links to impossibly cute pups on Petfinder.com.

But I remained unmoved. No, I said—no new puppy.

In the summer of 2008, Henry decided to take matters into his own hands. Despite my resistance, he was quietly adamant that it was time to get a new dog. And he wanted a bigger dog this time—"while we can still handle it," he explained—but one that would calm down over time. When we took our beach walks in Connecticut after Buddy died, Henry looked longingly at big dogs that fetched and swam. And he preferred a female on the theory that they are easier to manage.

Unbeknownst to me, Henry had fallen in love with a gentle golden retriever who belongs to two close friends of ours in Connecticut, an older couple named Marian and Howard Spiro. Henry particularly admired the perfect manners that the Spiros' dog—named Cyon, after Procyon, the brightest star in the constellation Canis Minor—exhibited in company.

Henry had become smitten during the ritual Sunday morning lawn bowling games when they were hosted by Dr. Spiro. (Most of the competitors were octogenarians, but Henry played to win and often did so.) During the games, Cyon would observe the bowlers placidly, never barking or chasing the ball. That September, at the Spiros' traditional Labor Day party, Cyon never once overtly begged, jumped up to catch a piece of stray cheese, or knocked over a gin and tonic.

Cyon, who is certified as a hospital therapy dog, has a regal stance and is an unusual, almost white color. From the Spiros we learned that she is a special type of golden retriever bred along British standards. Goldens are the second most popular breed in the United States, but until meeting Cyon we hadn't realized that they come in several hues, from deep red to the more common honey color, and finally to Cyon's platinum. By early fall 2008, Henry had become all but fixated on the notion that we should get an English golden retriever puppy, and he then began a gently insistent effort to persuade me to agree to this plan. My heart still ached for Buddy and I still wasn't sure I was ready for a new dog, but finally I consented.

After getting a referral from Marian Spiro, Henry contacted Donna Cutler, a breeder of English golden

Cyon on the beach in Connecticut

retrievers near Boston. Donna told him that she expected a new litter the following spring, and in December 2008, with my wary consent, he sent for an application and put down a deposit toward the price of one of the yet-unborn puppies.

I felt guilty. With millions of dogs in shelters across the country waiting to be adopted, and with local animal rescue groups actively looking for new homes for goldens who were given up or mistreated, I was aware that it would make more sense for us to adopt a dog rather than purchase a purebred puppy. Though far fewer dogs are euthanized in shelters than in past decades, about three to four million unwanted dogs are put down each year, according to the ASPCA. How could we justify getting a new puppy?

But Henry had his heart set. A puppy. A female. A blond golden retriever. By the following summer, I would be through with my physical rehabilitation, and Henry wanted a big water dog that we could train, play with at the beach and in the water, and settle down with as we cruised into our sixties. Because goldens need a great deal of exercise, Henry joked that he wanted to train her as a certified therapy dog—for us.

Once we had the application in hand, Henry suggested that we fill it out together. I still had a lot of concerns, including my big worry that I might never be able to love another dog as much as Buddy. I also worried that goldens have high rates of cancer and hip dysplasia, an inherited condition that sometimes shows up in X-rays of a puppy's parents, but not always. Donna had certifications for any number of health issues regarding all her dogs, although these certifications are never definitive. We also appreciated her insistence we sign a spay/neuter contract, something most reputable breeders require.

Donna was obviously committed to breeding a healthy litter of puppies; meanwhile, we were certain that we did *not* want to buy a puppy from a local pet shop, even if we found one that offered the fairly rare English golden retriever. Most commercial pet stores get their puppies from puppy mills, many of which are located in the Midwest, especially Missouri. The dogs in these mills are kept in cramped cages, lack proper medical care and nutrition, and often develop serious health problems. Millions of puppies are churned out by these notorious mills, and although the Department of Agriculture is supposed to inspect the mills and enforce the Animal Welfare Act, the USDA has few inspectors.

Some of the questions on Donna's application were a bit daunting; I felt almost as if we were applying to college. She asked how we rated ourselves on such things as the number of hours we would be leaving the dog alone during the day and the amount of time we would spend traveling. (In part because Henry works from home as a consultant, we were confident that we would be suitable owners.) We were asked to gauge our family's activity level on a scale of 1 to 10, with 1 being a couch potato and 10 being a triathlete. (Especially since we both love the outdoors, we declared ourselves a solid 7.) Donna's questions were valid because goldens thrive on lots of human company and need a great deal of exercise.

Her application also asked if we were prepared for constant digging and shedding. The digging wouldn't be a problem, but the question about shedding gave me pause, because on dark clothing the white hairs of this breed of retriever stand out, magnificently. After thinking it over, I decided that I was willing to put most of my black work clothes—basically my entire wardrobe—in the back of the closet. Besides, Henry and I are not the fussy *House Beautiful* types; our house and apartment both have dorm-room levels of disarray, perhaps reflecting the fact that we met in college and sometimes think it's still 1976. In the end only one question stumped me. Was our lawn "meticulously kept"? Well, it depended on your definition of *meticulous*.

As we completed Donna's application, I could feel my worries about getting a new dog melting away.

English golden retrievers have so many good characteristics: not only are they gorgeous dogs that love the outdoors; they are loyal, smart, and sweet-tempered. I also told myself that after meeting Donna, we could always change our minds. Or at least we could right up to the moment when we actually made contact with a real puppy. One lick on the face and I knew we would instantly be past the point of no return.

Donna accepted our application, but she wanted to interview us in person. So in May 2009, seven weeks after the new litter of English goldens was born, Henry and I drove from our house in Connecticut to Thistledown Golden Retrievers.

During the drive, Henry cruelly informed me that he was replacing me as pack leader because I am neither calm nor assertive, the qualities required by Cesar Millan, the famous dog behavior specialist. (We had watched Millan's television show, *Dog Whisperer*, on the eve of our journey.) There would be no human food prepared for our new dog (good-bye, grilled chicken). This dog, unlike the stubborn Buddy, was going to be well trained. "You are wonderful, but you don't know how to be firm," Henry said as we drove up I-95. "When Buddy would pull the leash so hard that your arm was on the verge of detaching, you'd giggle and say, 'Buddy, no,' and let him keep going."

Henry's assessment was harsh but fair. Although I could be tough and hold the line as a parent and as an editor at the *Times*, I was a pushover with Buddy. In my defense, we had both been so busy with the kids and work that we simply weren't able to devote the time needed to train Buddy properly.

Two hours after setting out, we arrived at Thistledown. We had expected Donna Cutler to look like a Scottish noblewoman, or at least one of those tweedy, stout women who show their dogs at the annual Westminster Dog Show. Instead, the woman who met us at the door was trim, with medium-brown hair, sharp features, and a friendly but down-to-business demeanor. Donna told us that she had just returned from showing one of her dogs in a competition in Canada. She competed in many shows up north, where the English golden retriever—with its unusual color, chunky head, and thick torso—is much admired.

Donna, who was then in her late forties, was still dressed in the pants suit she'd worn during the competition. We, by contrast, were in shorts and sneakers, hoping to emphasize our vigor and sportiness. As

Donna led us to the back of her house—which had big fenced-in pens for the adult dogs and another outside area for puppies—I was nervous and fearing rejection. (Later we learned that Donna had turned down a potential customer only twice. One was a gent who refused to commit to enclosing his yard so the puppy would be safe. The other was a woman in Donna's town who kept brushing the hairs off her coat during the first puppy visit.)

No doubt to put us at ease, Donna told us a bit about herself. She had grown up in Dedham, Massachusetts, where her family had pets of every kind, including wild baby rabbits, stray cats, and a bantam rooster that lived in the house so it wouldn't wake up the neighbors. But the family had only one dog, a pug that belonged to her grandmother. This pug, Donna told us, was simply "not fun." Moreover, pugs are small, and Donna wanted a big dog. For weeks, she and her sister saved up their allowance, and then one day they biked into town and bought a dog collar and a leash. Several times that summer, they rounded up a big dog that had been wandering around town, as dogs did back then. The two girls would drag it home to the garage and remove the collar and leash so as not to give away their gambit. Then they would go into the house and exclaim to their parents that a dog had followed them home. But each time, as soon

Tess and her litter of puppies, with Scout on the side

as the garage door was opened for an inspection, the pooch would bolt out of the yard and beat it back to town.

Donna had been breeding goldens for years, and the puppies' parents, grandparents, uncles, aunts, and great-grandparents still lived on the premises. (This is one of the signs of a reputable breeder, and most experts advise checking out the parents of a puppy for temperament, looks, and health history.) After we'd chatted for a while, she showed us around her yard. On the right, there was an area cordoned off by knee-high portable fences where Tess, the mother of the new litter, was lying down surrounded by her progeny. The nine puppies were not yet completely weaned and were the cutest little fur balls I had ever seen.

Donna explained that the puppies were becoming socialized by romping with one another under their mother's watchful eye. Once in a while, one pup would squeal when a brother or sister nipped an ear too hard. One of the most important things new puppies learn is how to moderate their bites. These pups already had their set of twenty-eight baby teeth, which were like sharp little razors.

There were four females in the litter, and I asked Donna if she had a particular one in mind for us. She said that because our life was split between the country and the city, she thought the smallest female

Scout under the green chair

might be best. But her tone when she answered was noncommittal, probably because she hadn't had a chance to observe us with the puppies. No seal of approval yet.

One of Donna's favorites in the litter was a tiny female she called Cindy Lou, named after the smallest denizen of Dr. Seuss's Whoville in *How the Grinch Stole Christmas*. The Seuss character had a yellow streak in her hair, and so did this puppy. We later learned that Donna also saw in this pup the kind of "attitude" that she believed was well suited for life in the big city.

I looked more closely at Cindy Lou. She was tiny, with sleepy eyes, and as some of her brothers and sisters nursed, she hovered under a green plastic chair. That worried me a little. Was this pup too shy?

"It's okay to pick them up," Donna told us. I cradled the little one in my lap. I was tempted to bring her up to my nose and take in the wonderful smell that all new puppies have; instead, since I knew that very young dogs absorb every new experience primarily through their noses, I let her get a good whiff of me.

Soon all the puppies, including this little one, perked up and wanted to play. Henry jumped into the pen and let them chase his heels. All of the pups had a different color ribbon around their necks so Donna could keep track of who was who.

Henry and the puppies

Tess, the mother, watched all this from a few yards away. She was a blond beauty who when she was younger was a potential champion. But one day, while Donna was in Wyoming on a girls' weekend, a stick had snapped back and sliced Tess's eye, which couldn't be saved by a veterinarian. Still, even with the closed, missing eye, she was a knockout.

Donna took us to the adult dog area to meet the father of the pups, a big boy named Patrick who had won a championship in Austria. Aside from his good looks and fluid movement—a sort of sashay that suggested powerful legs—Patrick was chosen to be this litter's father for his even temperament, a trait we hoped all the puppies had inherited. Donna also provided us health certificates showing that Tess and Patrick had been checked repeatedly for hip and elbow dysplasia but exhibited no signs of it.

After visiting with Donna and her dogs for two hours, we felt that we were beginning to trespass on our hostess's time. Before we left, Donna put tiny Cindy Lou and one other female pup in an indoor area so we (and, presumably, she) could be sure.

"So have you thought about a name?" Donna asked. (Clearly a hopeful sign!)

Yes, we had. Actually, Henry had been disqualified in the name-the-dog contest, because when I was pregnant the first time he had briefly considered giving

Cornelia the name Jemima. Two years later, Will almost became Ichabod. (Henry likes the old-fashioned names from his Puritan family tree. "If we don't use those names, who will?" he would ask, indirectly answering his own question.) But after frantic consultations with Cornelia and Will, we had decided on the name Scout after the spunky little girl in Harper Lee's *To Kill a Mockingbird*.

"Well, Scout can't come home with you for two weeks," Donna said, giving us a date and time to come retrieve our retriever.

We still weren't sure which puppy she meant. But as we walked back to the car, the shock of Donna's last words sank in. We had passed.

On the ride home, I kept thinking about the tiny puppy with the slightly worried expression. And I was slightly worried myself. While watching Donna's litter of puppies, memories of Buddy as a new puppy had flooded my mind. I still wasn't sure whether my heart was ready to replace him.

CHAPTER TWO

In June, when she was nine weeks old, Cindy Lou—aka Scout—was finally ready to join our family.

Remembering how convenient it was to have a backyard for Buddy's early housebreaking, we had decided to have Scout spend her first weeks with us at our home in Connecticut, where we usually spend weekends and part of the summer. An antique colonial—it was built in the 1700s—the house is on a quiet street with an ample lawn. Although both of us usually work in New York City during the week, we had adjusted our schedules so Scout could begin life as a country girl. Manhattan is easily reachable by train, and I planned to spend three days out of every week in

Connecticut as often as possible. Meanwhile, Henry could work from Connecticut during the summer and had in any case cleared his schedule of just about everything except puppy training.

While waiting for Scout's homecoming, we had spent a small fortune at Petco, one of the national pet supply chains. We needed a gate to close off our open and now rugless kitchen and family room area. Since Scout would be growing fast, we bought a giant bag of the same kibble that Donna had been feeding her, Purina Pro Plan for dogs with sensitive skin and stomachs. We also purchased a crate where she would sleep.

The aisles of every Petco, a company with an annual revenue of two billion dollars, are jammed with all manner of products, many aimed at humanizing dogs to an almost ridiculous extent, including five different models of puppy strollers, in colors like mango and sage. The sales associates refer to dog owners as "pet parents," which jibes with the times, as do the chain's other policies. Dogs are allowed inside the stores so they can shop with their parents, and Petco also offers a popular pet adoption service. The same Yuppie values that drove the explosive growth of designer products for infants, such as four-hundred-dollar Perego strollers and one-hundred-dollar ergonomic baby carriers, have now been transferred to pets. When Cornelia and Will were young, Henry and I didn't have the money to succumb to the marketing of these upscale baby products. But now we are empty nesters with a lot more disposable income.

Dog food, which used to come in two options, dry or wet, is now a cornucopia of choice, including special formulas for sensitive skin and stomachs and much higher-priced bags bearing "natural" and "organic" labels. Having edited stories about dubious health claims for expensive "organic" food for humans, I was skeptical upon seeing the same marketing techniques used by the seventeen-billion-dollar pet food business.

In Manhattan, I had visited several high-end pet boutiques, including one called Canine Caviar that sells thirty-dollar bags of "holistic" kibble. (There are also vegetarian, vegan, and kosher versions.) A few of our friends feed their dogs only raw food, another new dog food craze. And I also knew that some dog experts insist that it is healthier for dogs to eat only freshly cooked food. How could I possibly navigate this maze of options?

I consulted Marion Nestle, the author of several excellent books on human and pet food politics, including *Feed Your Pet Right*. Dr. Nestle believes that many of these exotic dog food formulas are just plain silly. She said that we should look for products labeled "complete and balanced," which indicate that they meet the nutritional guidelines for cats and dogs listed by the Association of American Feed Control Officials. Dr. Nestle told me that this organization—in conjunction with the Food and Drug Administration, state officials, and the animal feed industry—had developed pretty reliable regulations for pet foods. And she assured me that most of the commercial brands with these labels sold in supermarkets are fine for dogs, since almost all dog foods are made from the by-products of human food production. Paying attention to the basic ingredients is also advisable, she said.

It seems that almost every aspect of dog ownership has fierce, partisan battles lurking just below the surface. Perhaps the most contentious issue is whether a would-be dog owner should get a new dog through pet rescue and adoption or from a breeder. Upon hearing that Henry and I were getting a purebred puppy, several of our friends reacted as if we were buying a Hummer and thus doing something fundamentally bad for society. Cornelia had volunteered at a local animal shelter in Virginia, and we all understood that many dogs needed to be rescued and adopted. The horrified reactions seemed extreme.

Even dog toys provoke raging debates. We planned to put one of Cornelia's old stuffed animals in the crate to keep Scout company, fearing that she would be lonely once she was separated from her littermates. But nowadays, we were told, these are considered taboo because the synthetic stuffing could harm dogs if swallowed. Petco now offers flat plush toys without stuffing, but they look about as fun and reassuring as paper bags.

I tried to resist both the specious advice and the clever marketing ploys, but I wasn't entirely successful. During our shopping spree at Petco, I discovered that I liked the smell of Halo dog shampoo, which costs eighteen dollars for a sixteen-ounce bottle—a lot more than I pay for my own shampoo. While we stuffed our bags into the car that morning, I was still trying to figure out how our tab had come to four hundred dollars.

As we counted down to the big day, we felt jittery and underprepared, as if we were waiting for the arrival of a new baby. We knew that once tiny Scout was in our car, there would be no turning back.

When the day for pickup finally came, Henry and Will drove up to Thistledown while I stayed behind in Connecticut making final preparations. A little after three o'clock, Henry pulled into our driveway and there she was, a white ball of fluff resting in the backseat of our Subaru on an ancient Superman towel from Will's toddlerhood. Picking her up, I put Scout on the lawn and she padded toward the house. Halfway to the door, she squatted to pee. We clapped in jubilation, and we could scarcely believe our good fortune when she repeated this same routine a few hours later.

Scout seemed to be more than partly housebroken, an unanticipated gift from Donna. It was hilarious watching her trot out the back door onto the lawn; since her back legs were taller than the rest of her, she looked like she might topple over, which she sometimes did. She would scamper a ways and then randomly plop down. Scamper then plop, her legs betraying her as often as they propelled her forward.

Now that Scout was finally home, none of us could stop picking her up to cuddle. I had forgotten how much having a new puppy is like having a new baby. Besides looking for any excuse to inhale that irresistible puppy smell, I felt a reflexive urge to cover the top of Scout's soft head with kisses. It is actually very important for a new puppy to get used to being handled, but I admit that I wasn't kissing and cuddling with her because I knew it was the right thing to do.

Just as I did when our children were little, I made up lullabies with silly lyrics and then sang to her when she cried before sleep. I also felt the unparalleled joy of seeing her tired eyes close, although she would invariably wake again in the middle of the night. Henry, ever the hero, slept next to Scout's crate so that he could hear her stir when she needed to go outside to relieve herself. More than fifteen years had passed since we had performed this routine with Buddy, and we were rusty.

Scout woke every morning at six on the dot. She immediately started crying and whimpering, but she always cheered up the minute she had company. Cornelia, who had a few weeks of summer break from medical school, had come to Connecticut to help, and we traded off the responsibility for taking care of Scout in the early morning. When it was my turn, I didn't mind at all. The soulful brown eyes that greeted me had long lashes that gave Scout a sultry, flirtatious look; she was a canine version of Veronica Lake, down to her blond, silky fur. Although dogs supposedly don't like to be stared at, Scout looked deeply into my reddened, sleep-deprived eyes as if searching for clues. Who was this person? What were all these new smells?

She liked clamping down on my forearm with those needle-sharp teeth. Soon she was chewing on little rawhide bones, and she went through them like jelly beans. We watched carefully while she chewed, hoping we could prevent her from swallowing any of the pieces she worked so hard to detach.

Will's Superman towel now lined the bottom of Scout's crate, and Henry planned to buy a clock to put in the crate with her. He remembered that his mother, Lynne, had told him a story from her childhood about preparing a little bed for her new puppy, Nicky. Nicky slept in a laundry basket filled with soft, clean blankets, into which Lynne tucked an old-fashioned wind-up alarm clock. When Henry had asked her why she put the clock in the basket, Lynne answered, "The ticking reminded Nicky of her mother's heartbeat." This story was especially meaningful to Henry because his mother had died in her sixties of heart trouble.

Scout looked awfully little in her crate, but her big paws were a tip-off that she wasn't going to stay small. While she slept, I loved watching her little back as it rose and fell. Even so, I still sometimes worried that I might not love Scout as much as Buddy, a fear I kept to myself. I didn't know it then, but this is a very common worry of new dog owners.

It's also not unusual for new dog owners to be reminded of their experiences with infants. In fact, our response to a puppy may be partly hormonal. John Homans, who wrote a perceptive article about dogs and their owners for *New York* magazine, noted that a recent study showed that a dog's gaze increases oxytocin levels in its owner, and oxytocin is the same

Jill and Scout soon after Scout's arrival in Connecticut

hormone that creates such intense bonding between a baby and its mother.

It's long been understood that puppies stir powerful feelings in humans; in fact, over the thousands of years that dogs have been domesticated, breeders have purposely preserved their puppy characteristics, which is one reason why so many older dogs act like perpetual puppies. Temple Grandin, a widely respected animal behaviorist who raised many golden retrievers earlier in her life, was one of several experts I consulted during Scout's early puppyhood. She told me that breeders have also bred dogs to be hypersocialized. "So it's natural," Grandin said, "that some people treat their dogs like children. And the dogs are very attuned to us." Grandin, who is autistic, has written a number of books, and I found one of them, *Animals Make Us Human*, especially useful.

I consulted a number of other books as well. Next to Grandin's book on our shelf was a volume by the monks of New Skete, guide-dog trainers who lived in an Eastern Orthodox monastic community in upstate New York. The monks have written several extremely readable and useful dog-training manuals, including *The Art of Raising a Puppy* and *How to Be Your Dog's Best Friend*. I was amused one day when I realized that Henry and I used these books the same way our parents had turned to Dr. Spock to help raise us.

The monks' general precepts made a lot of sense to us, and their daily regimen for new puppies comported with our idea of how a day with a dog ought to go. Passionate advocates of a rural life, the monks were so persuasive on the subject that Henry decided to stay in Connecticut right through Labor Day, when Scout would be almost five months old. By then she would have had all her shots, which was not a small matter. City pavements can expose puppies to parvo, giardia, and other ailments that can potentially kill them overnight. The green of our backyard seemed a much safer option than the urban wilds of Manhattan.

Part of the plan for getting a dog precisely in mid-June was that the weather in Connecticut was likely to be lovely. With any luck, the pestilential heat and humidity of recent summers would hold off until Scout and we got our legs under us. Unfortunately, that's not how it worked out: instead of sweet spring gliding into summer, the weather was almost tropical and there were sudden thunderstorms nearly every day. Happily Scout showed no fear of the storms, but as she got bigger and feistier we all began to go stir-crazy. By the end of June, it was time for Scout to begin socializing with other dogs and with people. And it was time for us to emerge from our puppy bunker, too.

Our friend Marian Spiro came to our rescue. Ever since Scout's homecoming, Marian had been calling us frequently to check in and offer tips. Because her English golden retriever, Cyon, was Henry's inspiration for finding Scout, Henry considered every morsel of advice from Marian extremely valuable. At eighty-four, she had raised many puppies, including goldens, and she knew how to handle almost every challenging situation.

Now Marian invited Henry and Scout to join her and Cyon at four o'clock every afternoon so Scout could get to know Cyon and begin to learn some social skills. Marian filled an eight-foot-long baby pool in her backyard for the dogs to splash in, and the afternoon pool party soon became the high point of the day. Although Scout was still too little to climb into the pool, Marian gently introduced her to the water and she took to it right away.

A longtime friend of Marian's—an older gentleman named Clyde Campbell who spoke with a honey-eyed North Carolina drawl—would frequently join the pool party with his dog, Bunny. Another white golden with a rambunctious temperament, Bunny would sometimes splash too energetically in the pool or stomp on Marian's flower beds. "Bunny, no!" Clyde would shout in frustration. Gleefully, Henry called me at the office to tell me that he had new best friends, a couple named Bunny and Clyde.

Dog play can be utterly fascinating, a dance of dominance and submission, engagement and disengagement. At first, the new puppy in their midst interested Cyon and Bunny, but they were accustomed to being a sisterhood of two, and for the most part Scout was happy to watch them from the sidelines while sitting near us. Scout found the two big goldens especially entertaining when they both clamped their teeth on the same tennis ball and held it between them as if in a trance, their bodies in perfect tension for as long as five minutes. Scout knew not to try to get into the middle of that game, but as time went by she began to chase the bigger dogs. When she'd catch their attention, she would quickly lie down on her back in submission, showing her adorable white belly.

Learning to play with other dogs is about much more than having fun; in fact, it's probably the most crucial aspect of puppy development. In *Animals at Play*, Marc Bekoff, a biologist and animal behaviorist, describes the rituals of dog play, including the bow— front legs stretched forward, hips raised—that signals an invitation to play, and the subtle cues that warn another dog that the playing has turned too rough.

"Play is how dogs become card-carrying members of their species," Bekoff told me when I called to consult him.

Alexandra Horowitz's *Inside of a Dog: What Dogs See, Smell and Know* includes a wonderful description of a Chihuahua and a wolfhound playing together with total ease, despite their enormous size difference. "These dogs are so incommensurable with each other that they may as well be from different species," she writes. "The wolfhound bit, mouthed and charged at the Chihuahua; yet the little dog responded not with fright but in kind."

Next to full-grown Cyon and Bunny, Scout must have felt like a Chihuahua, but gradually she began to learn how to hold her own. When we walked down our street and let her off the leash in a nearby field, she would cower, tail between her legs, when Bacci, a huge Bernese mountain dog who belonged to a neighbor, approached her to play. Then, when he came up to her, Scout would run for the hills. But after a few minutes, she would return to Bacci and give him a few tentative sniffs. Soon they were playing like the Chihuahua and the wolfhound, just as Horowitz described it.

But it was Marian who remained the touchstone of Scout's early socialization, and they quickly formed a mutual adoration society. Marian has piercing blue eyes and a wonderful laugh, and when Scout was around we heard that laugh often, because Marian seemed to be amused by just about everything Scout did.

We had known Marian and her husband, Howard, casually for many years. Henry and their son, Chip, were roommates in college, and we would often run into Marian and Howard at the beach and around town. But we got to know them much better when I started teaching a course at Yale, where Howard is an emeritus professor of medicine. After a couple of chance meetings on the commuter train, Howard invited us to become associate fellows of one of Yale's colleges, and later he inducted Henry into the Lawn Bowling Association. Marian and Howard have extensive professional networks and a hectic social schedule, but they never let you know it. As a friend of ours remarked upon meeting them over lunch, they possess "not a single drop of pretension between them."

Everyone in the Spiro clan is an avid sailor, and the mix of dogs and the sea comes naturally. One granddaughter wrote for a grade-school class exercise, "I love my Grandma because she has a big dog and a big boat." Howard, who has a deep voice and a penchant for aphorisms, often notes that "there's nothing better for a cut than saltwater and dog saliva."

Unlike many people with goldens, Marian came to the breed later in life. She grew up during the

Depression in Fall River, Massachusetts, and her family owned a succession of cocker spaniels. "They ran loose, as all dogs did back then," she recalled. Even before she and Howard had children, they got a mutt. When she brought it back from the dog pound, the puppy was so small that it could fit in her pocket. Over the years, she had a series of pound puppies until one of them mated with a golden, at which point they became smitten with the breed.

The Spiros have owned three goldens, and all three were named after stars or constellations. First came Orion, then Sirius, and now there's Procyon, or Cyon for short. Sirius became famous for accompanying Marian to the science class she taught at a private middle school in New Haven. The dog would rest quietly in his crate during class but then come out so that the kids could pat him while coming and going.

Despite the celestial monikers of her dogs, Marian's dog-raising philosophy is down-to-earth. "Dare I say it's just maternal instinct?" she said to me, reassuringly. Key to her approach is the element of patience, for both dogs and their owners. Very early on in Scout's life, Marian would hold a piece of high-value treat, like a small piece of cheese, mere inches from her snout and say, "Wait . . . wait . . . wait, baby." Only when Scout was calm and sitting still would Marian deliver the goody. Marian repeated this ritual several times a day.

Other puppies would practically bite off a finger while trying to get the snack, but Scout learned to hold back and resist temptation, which served us well in our later training work.

At some point we learned that Marian, Clyde, and their dogs are charter members of a dog-walking group that meets at 7:30 a.m. most mornings, even in winter, at a town-owned farm near our house. In mid-July, after Scout received the puppy shots due when she turned thirteen weeks old, Marian and Clyde invited us to join the group. The point of this morning session is to give the dogs exercise by letting them gambol, without leashes, in the acres of lush meadowland owned by our town. The pristine white farmhouse, the ponds filled with flowering yellow water lilies in spring through fall, and the old covered wooden bridge on the property make it look a lot like one of those gorgeous Monet paintings.

On any given morning in July, we saw as many as a dozen dogs walking off-leash with their owners. Besides Cyon and Bunny, the regulars included Olive, a black pug whose smushed face made it hard for her to breathe in the summer heat; Sadie, an older Airedale; and Viggo, a huge, seven-month-old German shepherd who was being trained by a woman named Lee Gibson to become a seeing-eye dog for the blind. Lee had agreed to give Viggo a loving home and his early puppy training, but when he turned a year old he would be leaving her to begin his formal training in a guide-dog program. Lee also had an extremely shy Japanese chin named Zen, who sometimes walked with us but usually preferred to wait by himself next to Lee's car.

These daily outings taught us far more about how to raise Scout than the monks and our other books did. Lee, for one, knows an enormous amount about dogs and was a fount of training tips. The visits to the farm socialized us, too. Clyde instructed us to guard our knees when the dog pack came running our way. "You could blow out a knee and wind up in the hospital again, Jill," he warned me. He also encouraged me to buy a pair of Muck Boots like his to keep my feet dry in the mornings, when the grass was still covered with dew.

Following the death of the film director John Hughes that summer, we dubbed our little group of early morning dog walkers the Breakfast Club. Especially if Scout had had one of those nights when she needed to be let out a lot, I was often exhausted, but I cherished those morning meetings. Soon I could match the cars to the pet owners, and I would be disappointed if we drove up to the parking area and didn't immediately see any of our friends.

Day by day, Scout became bolder—and bigger. "Scout, you've grown another six inches," Clyde would exclaim nearly every morning, and it almost seemed true. She was eating like crazy, gulping down her kibble with a frosting of yogurt and gaining about half a pound a day. When she arrived in Connecticut in mid-June, Scout had weighed sixteen pounds; by late July she weighed almost thirty pounds. As she grew, Cyon, Bunny, and the rest of the pack sternly enforced what Scout could get away with (joining them in chasing rabbits) and what she couldn't (dashing into the pile of discarded vegetables). Sometimes the other dogs were plainly annoyed by this overeager puppy who followed their every move and tried to steal their balls. Viggo could be particularly grouchy, and sometimes he would turn on Scout and give her a "stay away from me" growl. But though Scout clearly didn't enjoy this sort of rejection, she needed to learn how to interpret social cues.

Marian continued to be amused by Scout's wild and ungainly strides, but her demeanor around all the dogs was relaxed yet firm. If Cyon began to race off into the woods, Marian would immediately call her back. A sharp "Cyon, come!" would result in the prompt reappearance of her dog. If Bunny and Scout had followed Cyon, they would dawdle behind her with mildly guilty expressions. Afterward, Marian would get all three dogs to sit and take out her bag of small treats. "Wait," she'd tell them, wanting to encourage soft mouths and keep them sitting. Only then would she give them each a treat. The Breakfast Club ended each morning with Marian inviting all three white goldens into the back of her car, where she split her last treat three ways.

We copied the Marian technique at home, getting Scout to sit and be patient before bestowing a treat for good behavior. We faithfully spent part of each day training Scout, helping her to learn her name and a few basic commands. Henry also made a point of giving her a ride in the car as often as possible, which at first provoked a lot of howling and braying until Scout finally realized that getting in the car usually meant a trip to Marian's or doing something else fun. And in preparation for Scout's eventual arrival in New York, Henry would take her in the afternoon for rides up and down the elevator at the local commuter train station.

Scout usually spent her downtime in the giant stand of lilacs just beyond our kitchen door, which Henry had enclosed with chicken wire. Aside from providing shade all day, the fenced-in area around the lilacs gave Scout the opportunity to explore her own

Bunny (left), Cyon (center), and Scout (right)
in the back of Marian Spiro's car

little forest, bury toys, and chase Henry as he ran around the perimeter. One fine morning Scout was napping in the lilacs and Henry was reading nearby when a UPS deliveryman arrived. "Must be nice," the man remarked as he handed Henry the package. And, indeed, it was very nice.

～～～

Because my job as managing editor of the *Times* required that I spend most weekdays in my New York office that summer, I called Henry each afternoon to hear the latest news from his and Scout's farm walk or Marian's pool parties. Finally, in early August, I couldn't stand missing so much of the fun and took a two-week vacation.

I was elated by the prospect of spending an uninterrupted stretch of time with Scout. I was also eagerly awaiting the visit of my friend Mariane Pearl and her seven-year-old son Adam. Mariane was the widow of Danny Pearl, the *Wall Street Journal* reporter who had been my friend and colleague in the *Journal's* Washington bureau. Adam was the son Danny had never met, since Danny had been kidnapped and murdered in Pakistan by al-Qaeda while Mariane was pregnant.

Adam loved the beach, superheroes, baseball, and

dogs. He was excited to meet our new puppy, and I was anxious for Scout to learn how to behave around a child, since Buddy had sometimes growled at visiting toddlers, which scared them and alarmed me. When the Pearls arrived in Connecticut from New York, Adam brought Scout a Yankees dog shirt as a gift and was determined to teach her how to play left field in Wiffle ball games.

Under Adam's tutelage, Scout became an extremely fast and adept outfielder, but she never got the hang of dropping the ball after she caught it. In my dual role as pitcher and mediator, I would usually have to negotiate a trade, giving her a treat in return for the ball.

It was on this field of dreams that Scout had her first big mishap. One sweltering afternoon, she took her customary position in far left field. As I pitched and Adam endured a long series of balls, hitless swings, and foul tips, sap from a pine tree dripped all over Scout. When Adam saw what had happened, he cried out, "Scoutie looks like a dalmatian!" She was a terrible, sticky mess, and after dragging her into the house I scoured the Internet for remedies. Once I discovered the recommended treatment, I dabbed the spots of tar with olive oil and peanut butter. By the end of this tedious process, Scout was once again blond, but she smelled like a peanut butter sandwich.

Our house wasn't far from Long Island Sound,

and during Adam's visit we often took Scout for walks on the beach. She was wary of the surf, but she liked to splash along the shoreline and let the water rise up to her belly. We were all thrilled when Adam threw a stick and Scout dove in, retrieved the stick, and paddled back to shore. Then she wouldn't give up the stick, but we nonetheless celebrated the superb display of her retriever roots. Scout and Adam got along famously, and it warmed my heart to watch the two of them—these two beautiful puppies—cavort in the sand and the sea. By the end of Adam's visit, I was pretty certain that Mariane would be dealing with a major episode of "Can we please get a dog" begging when she and Adam returned to Paris.

The Monday after Mariane and Adam left, my vacation came to an end. That morning, as I dressed in my office clothes, I felt as if I were assuming another identity, much as I did when I went back to work after maternity leaves. While riding the Metro-North train from New Haven to New York, I began making the transition back to my life at the *Times* by reading the papers and catching up on e-mail.

With the vacation behind me, I plunged back into my job and stayed in the city for two full weeks. This was my first extended separation from Scout, and it was a little depressing to live a solitary life again. As a new puppy owner, I had made so many new friends, both dog and human, and over the summer I had become much calmer and happier. I missed the morning walks with the Breakfast Club, which felt like a much healthier way to start the day than rushing to my computer. Most of all, I missed Scout. Bill Keller, my boss and the paper's executive editor, told me that he noticed a sudden rise in the number of dog stories being pitched for the front page. To curb the trend, he urged me to recuse myself from any discussion about a proposed dog story.

Inevitably, I showed off my latest Scout photos to anyone who betrayed even a hint of interest. Over the years, my office had become a Buddy shrine; many of my friends and colleagues had deluged me with every kind of Westie item, from a needlepoint pillow to a white ceramic pen container. Michiko Kakutani, the *Times*'s chief book critic, was particularly generous: not only had she given me dozens of pairs of socks emblazoned with Westies; she had also given me an antique desk lamp with a bronze terrier perched on its base. It was made in the 1940s, when Scottish terriers were the rage because of President Franklin Delano Roosevelt's beloved dog, Fala.

Even after Buddy died, people who didn't know me

especially well kept sending me Westie gifts. Recently, I had tearfully opened a set of Westie coasters and then a white bar of soap in the shape of a Westie. So when I returned to my desk one day and found a package from the columnist Maureen Dowd, I worried that it, too, would contain more Buddy stuff. Instead, the box contained a ceramic plate with a golden retriever puppy painted on it. I displayed Maureen's gift in a place of honor, and now all the white in my office could begin to turn golden.

CHAPTER THREE

Chewing. It was a constant with Scout. Her needlelike baby teeth were being replaced by permanent, bigger ones and the teething was driving her nuts. At fifteen weeks, she had grown bored with our usual cache of rawhide bones and frozen towel bows and was now wild for shoes, preferably Cornelia's fanciest ones. We were vigilant, we thought, but Scout managed to chew and flatten beyond recognition a pair of black satin sandals with sassy bows that our daughter had carelessly flung into the gated family room and kitchen area where Scout slept in her crate, ate her food, and happily chewed. But even sequestered and puppy-proofed, the space offered a thousand temptations, from the cording on the couch upholstery to the wires of our computers. We lived in fear of puppy electrocution.

Partly so we could keep an eye on her, we removed one of the cushions from our couch and encouraged Scout to curl up in the resulting gap. This gave her a cozy place to sit within snuggle distance of us, and it was low enough that she could easily hop on and off. Dogs generally love protected spaces, and the sunken "nest" on the couch quickly became her favorite place to hang out.

One August evening, while we were enjoying a peaceful hour watching *Antiques Roadshow*, Scout climbed down from the couch and went behind it. As we watched the show, we were vaguely aware of what we assumed was the sound of Scout chewing on one of her rawhides, and she was really going at it. Then Henry got up to get a beer and saw, to his horror, that Scout had in fact been chewing on the leg of an old table, which was now completely covered with teeth marks. There was even a scattering of what looked like sawdust around the bottom of the leg.

Clearly drastic action was required, and we began by removing all the nearby wooden chairs and tables. Next we christened the area on top of her crate the Land of No; this became a no-chew zone, and whenever Scout stole a forbidden object we put it there. The roof of the crate soon resembled a clearance sale at Macy's, with layers of outlawed goods stacked up high. Meanwhile, Scout manifested her obsession with chewing outdoors as well. Clumps of grass clippings from the lawn mower, pinecones, and even shells at the beach were all grist for her new set of choppers.

I took some solace from the stories told to me by friends who had made it through the puppy chewing frenzy. Phyllis Goverman, my college roommate, told me that "chewing was almost the end for us." As a young puppy, Lola, her now one-year-old Lab, had shredded Phyllis's most comfortable chair, eating a large helping of the stuffing in the process. Lola had also savaged the linoleum floor in the kitchen, where Phyllis left her during the hours she was teaching. I also consulted with Anna Quindlen, a former *Times* colleague and friend, who had written a book I loved called *Good Dog. Stay.* Anna comforted me by recalling that her queenly Lab, Bea, was fascinated with paper as a puppy—valuable paper. "She once ate a refund check from the State of New York, and $400 in $20 bills," Anna reported in an e-mail meant to reassure me.

By late August, Scout was big enough to launch carefully planned raids on the Land of No. This prompted us to give up her puppy-sized crate and buy one that would suit her when she grew to full size. At four and a half months, she already weighed almost forty pounds and was still gaining weight rapidly. Donna Cutler had estimated that she would ultimately weigh sixty pounds, but by using my powers as a crack investigative reporter, I observed Scout's huge paws and deduced that Donna's estimate would almost certainly prove too conservative.

What to feed Scout, when to feed her, and how to begin more serious training to curb her irrepressible puppy habits—like chewing shoes or jumping up on guests—were sources of growing tension between Henry and me. Since her arrival, we had been feeding Scout the same kibble diet that Donna had started her on. But she was constantly hungry and would have happily eaten twice what we fed her. Meanwhile, Henry had instituted a ban on human food except for the yogurt on the kibble. He was determined that Scout not become the fussy eater and beggar that Buddy was, with his taste for grilled chicken or (I confess) salmon, preferably wild Alaskan sockeye. Our stern pack leader was quick to point out that Buddy had become so spoiled by this richer diet that he utterly spurned unadorned kibble, and it was true.

Henry had been overjoyed to note that during her earliest weeks with us, Scout had been indifferent to our family gatherings at the table, which I attributed to the new, stricter food rules. But one night she began barking excitedly while Henry was eating a bowl of strawberries with whipped cream. Funny, we thought, strawberries don't usually appeal to dogs. Then, as I was scattering cheese on top of a pan of lasagna, Scout went nuts as I shoved the pan into the oven. That night we put two and two together: these white toppings on our food looked like her yogurt.

The fatal connection—between our food and her always-hungry stomach—had been made. And once it was, she was always by our side at the table, pleading at us with those irresistible brown eyes and batting those big lashes. Soon she began barking at us while we were eating. When she wouldn't stop, we had to enforce time-outs and shut her in our laundry room while we downed a meal and listened, all of us miserable, to her pathetic whimpering.

In desperation, I called Jane Mayer, who had trained three Labrador retrievers, including Peaches, yellow and regal, for whom we occasionally dog-sat. Peaches was mellow about everything but food. Once, when I was in the kitchen baking a cake, a stick of butter was softening on the counter. In the instant I turned around to get the eggs out of the fridge, the butter was gone. Peaches had only a slightly guilty expression on her face.

"Food can be your friend," Jane told me. "It is a great reward. She wants to please you, and a treat will help you reinforce her good behavior. Stop focusing so much on what displeases you." Since working together on our book about Clarence Thomas, we often turned to each other for advice when we were covering tough stories or experiencing difficulties in our careers. "Jill, you handled Howell Raines," Jane reminded me, referring to a former *Times* executive editor with whom I had often clashed. "You can handle a puppy."

Henry's strict approach to feeding Scout began to bend when Marian Spiro, whom we considered the ultimate dog authority, agreed with Jane that puppy treats were useful for marking Scout's good behavior. "Use them when you are practicing basic commands like Sit, Stay, and Come," she urged us. Cyon's favorite, Marian told me during a walk at the farm, was Pup-Peroni, especially the "original bacon recipe." (It comes in a bright red package, and thanks to the pet food industry's slick marketing it looks pretty delicious.) When Marian offered my ravenous pup a little taste of the soft beefy treat, Scout's face reminded me of Cornelia's thrilled expression as a toddler when, against my better judgment, I let her have some Cheetos. From then on, whenever Scout saw us drop the red package of Pup-Peroni onto our kitchen counter after one of our regular shopping sprees at Petco, she recognized it immediately and practically toppled over in ecstasy.

⟨⟨⟨

As summer drew to a close, a deadline loomed: by Labor Day we had to finish preparing Scout for her introduction to Manhattan. I couldn't wait for her to join me in the city. After my two-week vacation in August, during which I had bonded much more intensely to Scout, I found the weekdays without her almost intolerable.

I knew the transition from Connecticut to New York wouldn't be seamless. For one thing, we couldn't assume that months of housebreaking in the country would carry over. Still, it had been many weeks since Scout had had an accident inside our house, so we were fairly confident that she would quickly learn to wait for an elevator before getting outside our building, though it might prove harder for her to become used to relieving herself on communal pavement instead of the grass on our lawn.

Before she became a part-time city dog, Scout needed to learn how to walk on a leash, and we had already begun practicing. As we moved along our street in Connecticut one day, I thought things were going pretty well until I felt a tug, looked behind me, and saw Scout on her back, her adorable belly exposed, snapping at the leash like a turtle. For her, the leash was simply another object begging for a good chew. More troubling, Scout invariably lunged if a squirrel or chipmunk crossed the road near us. I worried about how she would do crossing the busy, traffic-choked streets of Tribeca.

Sometimes we practiced walking her on a leash at the farm. After one long session during which Henry walked Scout while wearing wet, ill-fitting shoes, he developed painful tendonitis. Now, at least for the time being, I became Scout's sole leash instructor and my left leg—the one with the titanium rod in it—began to ache. Not surprisingly, our temporarily crippled state led me to have some nagging second thoughts about the wisdom of getting such a large puppy who needed so much exercise. The monks, wise though they are, had provided no advice in their books for our situation. There is no Official Puppy Handbook for fifty-somethings.

Despite our infirmities, we couldn't ignore our 6 a.m. alarm clock, which was the sound of Scout braying to be freed from her crate. Sore and cranky though we were, the sight of her jumping excitedly on her hind legs to greet us each morning brought instant joy. Her favorite game was grabbing a toy in her teeth and prompting me to chase her outside and onto the lawn to play tug-of-war, often in my pajamas. (A new puppy, I quickly came to realize, gave me an unassailable license to be ridiculous in public.) During our morning play, she sometimes forgot about the growing strength of her jaws and drew blood on my hands and forearms.

Right before the summer ended, I had to travel to the *Times*'s Washington bureau for a two-day business trip. I was worried about leaving Henry, who was still disabled, alone with Scout. I also knew I would miss her terribly. But work called, and so off I went.

That evening, when I called Henry to check on how things were going, he delivered an upsetting report. One of his clients was a nonprofit group in Connecticut, and he was racing to complete a proposal for the group in the next week or so. He was so consumed by Scout care that he was already tense about meeting the deadline; then, on top of that, he had made a truly awful discovery. Scout had chewed the frames and broken the lenses of his tortoiseshell glasses, which had slipped out of his pocket and onto the couch. "This is really more than I was prepared to handle," he moaned. Luckily, his optician was able to make a replacement pair and ship the glasses to him overnight. In the meantime, he was wearing prescription sunglasses at his desk in order to get some writing done.

I felt horribly guilty because I was out of town and unable to help. But I also had a deeper concern: Scout's puppy destructiveness seemed to be reaching unacceptable levels. It was time to get professional help.

What happened next was a loopy canine version of O. Henry's famous short story "The Gift of the Magi." On the same day and without telling each other, Henry and I both put in a distress call to the same dog trainer.

I liked Diane Abbott the minute I heard her voice. For every tale of woe I recounted, her reaction was an amused giggle. Diane offered a puppy kindergarten class in a nearby Connecticut town, and in his initial conversation with Diane, Henry had been so favorably impressed that he had booked a home consultation with her for the next Saturday.

I had watched enough Cesar Millan to know that owners, almost always more than their dogs, are the ones who need training. So in the days leading up to our meeting with Diane, I made a list of all the questions and anxieties about Scout that I wanted to discuss with her.

By then, Henry and I agreed that we had to train Scout more rigorously than we had trained Buddy. It embarrassed me to remember that Buddy had flunked out of dog-training class, in large part because we were not consistent in practicing with him. We had also waited too long: we hadn't signed him up for classes until he was three years old. Diane told us that she liked to begin training with pups as young as three months.

On the morning of Diane's visit, Scout and I waited near our driveway. The woman who emerged from a tan hatchback had blond hair and looked like an athlete; reaching into her backseat, she pulled out a heavy, overstuffed bag and lugged it over to us. Scout immediately focused on the bag, practically jumping inside. Diane giggled, just as she had on the phone, which put me at ease. "She smells all my goodies," Diane said. Scout happily followed Diane inside.

Diane spent most of the next two hours talking to Henry and me. Scout watched us attentively and was occasionally called upon for a demonstration. During that first consultation, we learned several invaluable lessons.

Diane was particularly insightful about the importance of positive reinforcement. Every time Scout did something we didn't like, we had been using stern voices and telling her "No." Instead, Diane said, we

Scout gets her first lesson from Diane Abbott

should focus less on correcting her negative behavior and more on rewarding her positive behavior. "Concentrate on what we want," Diane told us. "Don't give attention to what we don't like."

Diane also introduced us to the use of a training clicker. When Scout responded in the way Diane wanted—such as looking at Diane when Diane spoke her name—Diane marked the behavior with a click from a red and yellow plastic clicker. Then she immediately gave Scout a treat from a little pouch that she had attached to her belt. It was filled with bits of chicken, most of them no bigger than a fingernail. Using the clicker and her treats, Diane quickly succeeded in getting Scout to respond to a number of different commands. She offered rewards for every bit of good behavior and suggested that we do the same, even if the treat was just a piece of kibble.

When Scout jumped up on us, Diane urged us to turn to the side and look away. Better to ignore Scout for a few seconds rather than scold her, and then get her to sit, followed by a click and a reward. When Scout nipped too hard during play, Diane suggested that we say "Ouch," put our hands up, and stop play. Then, after a few seconds, we should resume playing. Diane explained that this is how puppies play with their littermates. When one gets hurt and squeals, play stops for a bit and then continues.

Diane also said she thought Scout might have become bored with her toys and suggested that we get her a Kong, a cylindrical rubber chew toy that can be smeared with peanut butter or filled with puppy treats and put in the freezer. "It can really keep dogs busy," she said. "It's fun and interesting for them to work at getting what's inside."

At mealtime, Scout had the bad habit of barking loudly as we prepared her bowl. Fortunately, Diane had a cure. She suggested that we ask Scout to sit before we put her bowl down and then reward her patience with a piece of kibble. "Nothing is free anymore," she said. "Always ask for a sit before you feed her. Then give a click and a treat." When we tried this approach the next time we fed her, the barking stopped immediately.

Diane, who believes that small amounts of human food are good for dogs, gave us a list of approved and forbidden ones. Yogurt, already in Scout's diet, was fine, along with carrot chunks, cheese, and a number of other foods. On the verboten list, because they could poison a dog, were grapes, raisins, macadamia nuts, and, oddly, nutmeg.

This advice, of course, ran contrary to Henry's human food ban. But after hearing more about Diane's commonsense attitude toward food and seeing Scout's eager response to Diane's tiny bits of chicken, Henry declared that Diane had changed his mind. In the wake of Diane's visit, our pack leader's rules underwent a rapid evolution. In no time, they changed from "No Treats Whatsoever" to "Treats at Special Moments" to "Treats Basically All The Time Unless Scout Is Biting You." I was thrilled, of course, and secretly I hoped that one day Henry would let me return to the stove.

Without being pushy, Diane also suggested that we sign up for her next puppy kindergarten class, a package of eight sessions on Tuesday nights during which Scout would learn basic commands and socialize with other pups about her age. At the beginning of the consultation, we had talked with Diane about our plan to introduce Scout to New York, and now she told us that she thought the classes would help us handle Scout in the city. Henry, bless him, declared that he was willing to arrange his schedule around the puppy class. Instead of returning to the city on Sunday, he would work from Connecticut the first two days of the week and then drive to New York with Scout after Diane's class on Tuesday night.

Before she left, Diane gave Scout some hearty farewell pats and the two of us a clicker. Our separate cries for help had been answered.

I didn't want to miss Scout's first day of school, so the following Tuesday I left work early and took the train to Connecticut. Diane had promised that the class would be fun, and it was impossible not to trust someone who signed her e-mails, "Warmest wags, Diane." But it had been eighteen years since our younger child piled onto the school bus for the first day of kindergarten, and I felt the same mixture of anxiety and hopeful pride as we drove with Scout to the town where Diane taught her classes.

What we didn't know then was that by showing us how to use a clicker during her home consultation, Diane had introduced us to a dog-training method known as positive training. Later, I learned of the battle that rages between trainers who favor a more coercive, pack-leader approach and those who prefer a positive reinforcement technique that usually uses a clicker or a familiar sound to mark desired behavior in dogs.

Cesar Millan, whose television show on the National Geographic channel is one of the most popular shows on cable, is the avatar of pack leaders. Another cable personality, Victoria Stilwell, is a persuasive advocate of positive training. Others are also gaining national reputations for their ability to teach positive training; among them is Karen Pryor, the author of several popular dog-training manuals, under whom Diane had studied.

As with child-rearing, dog-training experts sometimes make convincing cases for completely opposing
points of view. On the pack leader versus positive
training issue, I had no idea which side was right; con-
fusing the matter, the monks' books, which had served
as our primary source for puppy advice, combine
some of both approaches. When I found time to do a
bit of research of my own, one of the experts I consulted was Shawn Stewart, who has worked with all
kinds of dogs, including homeland security canine
defense units. Stewart told me that the right method
depends on individual considerations about the dog,
the owner, and the environment. As he put it, "No one
out there can say that any one method will fit any dog
or any owner." In the face of conflicting advice, this
seemed like a very sensible conclusion.

Instinctively, Henry and I leaned toward positive
training. Our preferred parenting method had been to
use encouragement, not punishment, to teach our
children good behavior. And since Scout seemed eager
to learn and responsive to instruction, we were happy
to try out Diane's clicker training. Besides, if Scout
attended all the puppy classes and passed the course,
she would earn a basic manners certificate from the
American Kennel Club, the organization that sponsors
the Westminster Dog Show at Madison Square Garden each year. She would officially be a Good Dog.

It took about twenty minutes to drive to Durham, a town just to the north of us. Diane's class met next to a veterinary clinic in a large commercial garage with high ceilings and roll-up doors. There were six other puppies in the class. At forty pounds, Scout was the largest pupil by far. Diane had the *humans*—she preferred this word to *owners*—and the leashed pups introduce themselves on the lawn outside the classroom. Because Scout had become well socialized with other dogs at Marian's pool parties and at the farm, she pulled eagerly toward her classmates.

Scout was especially smitten with a tiny Chihuahua named Petunia, who cowered each time Scout approached. Once inside the classroom, which had accident-proof concrete floors and was filled with colorful toys, Diane had to place a puppy fence around Petunia and her owner because the Chihuahua remained so shy and fearful. This only made Scout more besotted, and she expressed her ardor in loud, disruptive barking.

I could feel my face reddening, but Diane remained unfazed by Scout's yelps. "Just relax and have fun," Diane told me. She distracted Scout by inviting her to demonstrate an exercise called "charging the clicker," where the dogs practiced hearing the click, responding to it, and getting a treat. Diane had asked us not to

Puppy kindergarten class

feed the dogs before class so they would remain responsive to the treats.

Diane told us that she had become a devotee of the clicker method after she had attended a puppy class where a coercive trainer had dragged Diane's collie across the floor by her collar, practically choking her. "I wanted to find a different way," she explained. After attending one of Karen Pryor's training conferences, Diane met some other positive trainers in Connecticut and they began perfecting their techniques together. Not long after she gained certification from the Association of Pet Dog Trainers, she quit her job as the vice president of a plaster molding company to become a full-time trainer. "I felt this was my calling," she said.

Diane was a born animal lover, and no situation seemed to fluster her. She had always adored dogs, especially collies, and she enjoyed telling stories about the animals in her life. She had once trained a raccoon, Ziggy, who often palled around town with Diane's beloved collie, Ronnie, and her cat. One day the raccoon had lured Ronnie into the basement of a neighbor who had filled some shelves with jars of homemade raspberry jam. Ziggy climbed up and began smashing the jars on the basement floor. When the neighbor heard the noise and hurried down to the basement, he saw Ronnie's paws and face covered in red jam.

Ziggy had slithered away and Ronnie got the blame for the caper. Ziggy eventually returned to the wild, but she came back once with her three babies to show them off to Diane, who almost became teary when she told the story.

Scout was entranced by Diane, as were the other dogs in the class. Happily, the dogs all seemed to get along well. Ella, a black Lab who was about Scout's age, had a sweet disposition and was less barky and jumpy than our pup. A springer spaniel in the class was already remarkably well trained: her owners took turns getting her to sit, stay, and lie down on command, much to the chagrin of the rest of us. A boxer puppy named Oliver was true to its breed and spent most of his time on his hind legs, trying to grab another dog or a human leg with its front paws.

The veterinary clinic itself was located on a large corner lot, and Henry had noticed that most of the owners and dogs showed up a few minutes early in order to get in a little walk. It was obvious that each of us hoped our puppy wouldn't embarrass us by having an accident during class, even though the garage's concrete floor would be easy to clean.

Halfway through the first class, Diane called for playtime and told us we could take our puppies off the leash. Scout's attention turned to Ella, and they were wrestling when I heard a little yelp: Scout had nipped

Ella's ear. But I didn't think it was an accident, and I immediately thought of Beverly Cleary's irrepressible heroine Ramona Quimby, who, in her first days of kindergarten, had a hard time suppressing her urge to pull the "boing-boing" curls of another student. Like Ramona, who loved her patient kindergarten teacher, Scout was crazy about Diane and barked with jealousy when Diane fixed her attention on one of the other dogs in the class. She wanted Diane to belong to her alone.

The biggest lesson Diane imparted in the first class was that dogs are visual creatures who respond to many kinds of cues besides verbal ones. Training, she said, is not effective if an owner uses only verbal communication, and sentences with many words will only confuse a dog. Instead, we needed to learn to employ visual cues, using our faces, bodies, and hands. Diane showed us how to get our pups to sit by moving a hand slightly over and behind the dog's head. Scout wouldn't respond to this signal in class, but after a few days of practice she began sitting in response to the hand motion.

In later classes, Diane taught us how to prepare our puppies for the unexpected. She gave us a sheet with "The Puppy's Rule of Twelve," encouraging us to expose our dogs to twelve different objects, people, and locations in the coming weeks. In one class, she made us put on funny clothes and carry canes and umbrellas. Another time, to help the pups learn to deal with sudden noises, she intentionally let a metal chair fall to the ground and make a loud clang. Henry and I were especially grateful for this phase of the training, since it would help prepare Scout for all the noise and strange people she would soon encounter in the city.

One of the most useful and gratifying exercises involved the command Leave it, which would later prove essential when Scout picked up something truly yucky on the streets of New York. (It still made us anxious to recall Buddy's uncanny ability to scour the city's sidewalks and find chicken bones, which can lodge in a dog's throat.) The premise was simple enough: Diane instructed us to present our puppies with a low-value treat, such as a piece of kibble or a packaged liver treat. When our dog turned her head toward it, we said "Leave it" and presented a far more appealing, high-value treat, like a bit of chicken. Scout responded to this command on the second or third try, and she got better at it within minutes, despite the tumult all around her. Food was a bigger motivator than we had imagined.

Like Buddy, Scout resisted the command Down, which is supposed to prompt a dog to lie on its belly. (We had better luck with Off, which we used in the early days to break Scout of her habit of jumping up on people.) When she saw that Scout wasn't responding to Down, Diane suggested that Henry sit on the ground and lure Scout under his knees with a treat. At the moment her belly touched the floor, Henry delivered a click and a treat. This exercise was especially valuable because it illustrated the need for creativity and persistence in the face of the challenges dogs always present.

As we learned more about dog training we realized that, although we had started late with Buddy, we had been wrong to give up on him. This time Henry and I vowed to stay the course, and we even set up a few between-classes sessions with Diane. During one such tutorial, Diane spent an hour with me on the road in front of our house teaching me how to pull Scout along on a leash. Though I was an attentive student, Scout was not. She alternated between nipping at the leash and trying to pull ahead of us when she saw something interesting.

As Diane's classes continued, I found myself, once again, immersed in the early education of a family member. Scout made rapid progress, and at some point I admitted to myself that I was hell-bent for my brilliant pup to earn her American Kennel Club basic puppy manners certificate. As part of a generation obsessed with getting our kids into the right schools,

I recognized that I was taking these puppy classes a little too seriously. But when Diane told me, "Scout is trying so hard to be a good dog, and I'm sure she'll get her certificate," parents everywhere would have appreciated the mixture of pride and relief I felt. And luckily for Henry and me, after Scout passed kindergarten, we wouldn't have to worry about her getting into college.

CHAPTER FOUR

Now five months old, Scout was completely house-broken, well socialized with all kinds of dogs and people, and the delight of our lives. Our summer of Scout had been full of stresses, but whenever I took a moment to watch her be a puppy in full—paddling in the waves of Long Island Sound or racing for Louis the Lobster (a favorite toy) so that we could play a morning game of chase—I knew we had been right to bring this loopy bundle of energy and love into our lives. When I wasn't with Scout, I missed her. When she was by my side, I felt happy and connected. A walk with Scout was always a good excuse to get outdoors and get outside of myself. And even though she no longer had the floppy ears and irresistible soft fur common to all very young puppies, I couldn't go anywhere with Scout without being stopped by someone who wanted to inquire about her breed or remark on her gorgeousness.

Goldens are known to be great family dogs because of their sweetness and their love of human company. Buddy had been much more independent. He liked to sleep downstairs, near our front door, and he actually preferred being left alone as long as he could patrol our yard and chase critters away. (Westies were originally bred to hunt rats.) But Scout rarely let us out of her sight and liked to curl up at our feet. Lately we had begun allowing her to sleep outside her crate, and sometimes, in the middle of the night, she bounded upstairs to check if we were still there and to give me a lick on my face. "She's a bigger presence than Buddy was," my sister observed one day. "She's needier and more human-focused than Buddy was."

But we were needy, too. After the departure of our children, Buddy's death, and my accident, our home lives had become a little narrow and thin. A new day didn't always bring a fresh store of energy and excitement, nor did we have anyone to baby or spoil. When Scout arrived, she undoubtedly began taking a lot of emotional cues from us, and she eagerly filled the spaces in our lives that used to be dedicated to our kids and, in recent years, had been filled up by work, going to the gym, and other activities that we each did separately.

Thanks to Scout, Henry and I were doing more together as a couple. We took long walks with her and often planned special outings we knew she would delight in, like hiking on the trails near our house in Connecticut. Henry and I had been together for more than thirty years by the time Scout came into our lives. Both caretakers by nature, we had enjoyed having various members of our extended families and friends of our children live with us for lengthy periods at different points during our long marriage. Bringing into our empty nest another living being to make happy and care for of helped put our relationship back on its natural axis.

Scout still attended Marian's pool parties almost every afternoon, and as she grew bigger and more confident in the water the hour at Marian's was usually followed by a visit to the beach. She never tired of dashing into the waves to retrieve sticks or balls. When she swam back to shore carrying her prize in her mouth, her very earnest expression always made us laugh.

More than anything else, she loved swimming into deep water with one of us, though we had to teach her not to scratch us with her front paws. She learned that when we said "Turn" she should swim away from us. She absorbed verbal cues quickly, and I taught her to swim laps in the ocean and stay in her own lane. When I said "Race," she would pick up her pace and almost always beat me across an imaginary finish line. This was terrific exercise for both of us.

But now the waters of Long Island Sound were cooler and summer was coming to an end. September often brings a crush of news, which I love. It gives the *Times* a back-to-school atmosphere after the sometimes quieter days of summer. I was a bit worried, though, that Scout-time would eat too much into my work. Somehow Scout seemed to sense this: in the morning, she patiently allowed me to sit at my computer to check the headlines and drink a cup of coffee. But then she would approach with one of her toys and head to the door, indicating that it was time to go outside and play. She was particularly attached to a toy called Crazy Henrietta, an indestructible rubber chicken wearing a purple and white polka-dotted bikini. With Henrietta in her mouth, Scout was pretty much impossible to resist.

September also meant that it was time to introduce Scout to Manhattan. We had always planned to bring her into the city after Labor Day; besides, Henry was working on a big report that was due at the beginning of October, and he needed to be in New York for the final writing and editing. We knew the transition would be difficult for her. Beyond our house and yard, the only places she had known were Marian's backyard, the farm, and the beach.

We planned to drive with Scout to New York right after Labor Day weekend. On the night of our departure, we invited the Spiros over for an early dinner of Italian sausages in a stew with white beans. This was their first visit to our house since Scout's arrival, and Scout was giddy with excitement when Marian walked in. Henry had to sternly insist that Scout not jump on our older friends, but the Spiros seemed little bothered by Scout's exuberance. When everyone was finally seated in our living room, Scout lay down at Marian's feet.

"I love what you have done with this dog," Marian said as I beamed with pride. Since Marian was so good at relating to dogs, her approval meant everything to me. But I knew the biggest test of Scout's newly acquired puppy manners would come when we sat down to eat. I silently prayed that she would not disrupt our meal with begging or barking.

Amazingly, she was perfectly behaved during dinner. Once again, she lay down obediently near Marian. Nothing, not even the tantalizing aroma of the stew, disrupted her tranquil demeanor.

When we had finished the main course, I cleared

the table and left the dishes—including a platter with a few leftover sausages—perched on a counter behind Marian's chair. Just then, Scout stirred, and before I could stop her, she hoisted her front paws onto the counter and, with lightning speed, jumped up and snatched a sausage. To my horror, Marian had witnessed the theft.

"Oh, that is very bad," Marian muttered, but then she couldn't help but giggle. "It's really our fault for putting such temptation within reach and not watching Scout carefully." She looked at Scout and said, "You are trying really hard to be good, baby."

After we said good-bye to the Spiros, Henry and I gathered up a few last things. We had already packed Scout's crate, a large bag of dog food, a pile of toys, food bowls, and other basic dog equipment. As the three of us piled into the car, I felt as if we were getting into a moving van. Happily, Scout seemed perfectly at ease. Except for her homecoming to Connecticut in June, Scout had never been on a long car ride, but she slept for most of the two-hour trip to Manhattan.

While Henry unloaded everything in front of our building, I took Scout for a walk. I hoped she would relieve herself, but she alternated between pulling on her leash to chase leaves and stopping dead on the pavement. I had forgotten how few actual patches of grass there are in downtown Manhattan. Moreover, the trees in front of our building are surrounded by two-foot-high wrought-iron fencing to keep dogs off of them.

Once inside our building, Scout sniffed everything nervously. She was reluctant to go inside the elevator, but we pushed her in. On the fourth floor we led her down the hall to our loft apartment; foolishly, we hadn't made the time to do any proper puppy-proofing or cordon off forbidden areas. As soon as we opened the door, Scout bounded straight for our room and did something she never did in Connecticut: she jumped on our bed.

This wasn't just any bed. It was a Swedish Duxiana bed, certainly the most expensive piece of furniture in our apartment. With its customized spring mattress and down topper, the bed had been a lifesaver after my accident, when finding a comfortable position for sleeping with a shattered left leg proved almost impossible. Everyone, including my doctors, encouraged us to buy the Dux, though initially we resisted such a costly luxury. Now, I watched in silent horror as Scout did something else she had never done: she squatted on the bed and peed, a big "I've been holding it for two hours" pee.

Henry and I rushed to the bed, and fortunately we were able to get the topper off before the lower mattress was saturated. After a rigorous washing by hand, the topper was clean again. By the time we all settled down for sleep, we were exhausted. But the street noise outside our windows rattled Scout, and she had a hard time getting to sleep and staying asleep. Like most puppies, she was frightened by the unfamiliar sounds and the barrage of new smells.

The next day, Henry got little work done at home because he was preoccupied with the effort to anticipate when Scout needed to go outside. Understandably, she hadn't yet learned to go to our door and bark, which is what she did in Connecticut. As a result, he was constantly on high alert, watching for any move Scout made that resembled the beginning of a squat, and often mistaking a sit for something more alarming. It was a little like being a new father again, when he would lie awake listening for his newborn's cry to be fed. By the time I came home from the office late that evening, Henry was crabby and anxious about his deadline. "This isn't working," he said, before shutting himself in our bedroom to do some reading, away from Scout.

I put down my things and looked at her. She was happily dozing, having recently eaten her dinner. I remembered Jane Mayer's wise words: "She wants to please you." If we insisted that Scout spend part of her week in Manhattan, I knew she would eventually learn to like it. Besides, she had learned so much during her three months in Connecticut. But I knew it would be hard for her to be a city girl when she had been such a happy country girl.

Taking a cue from all the movies about girls arriving in the big city for the first time, I decided that it would probably help if Scout met a savvy city friend. She could be the canine version of another one of my favorite blondes, Jean Arthur, who in the film *Easy Living* plays a plucky, working-class gal who follows Ray Milland to the fancy penthouses of New York swells and finds true love and good fortune.

The only handsome guy I knew who lived in an almost-penthouse was Charlie, a tiny black and white Havanese who belonged to my pal and neighbor Ellen Pollock. Although it was already 10 p.m., I called Ellen, who had worked with me for years at the *Wall Street Journal*, and convinced her that she and Charlie needed to join us on a late night stroll. Since they lived right across the street on the thirty-fifth floor of an apartment building, they joined us on Greenwich Street not five minutes later. Scout joyously began sniffing Charlie, who was a twentieth of her size.

We walked toward the river and soon passed a neighborhood dog run that Ellen and Charlie frequented.

The lights were still on and, since it was a hot night, so was a sprinkler. There was also a wading pool, so even if this wasn't Marian's pretty backyard, I hoped that Scout would find the water familiar and fun. Sure enough, the second I unleashed Scout she ran straight to the water.

While Ellen and I caught up on journalism gossip, Scout and Charlie splashed and played in the water. Their huge size difference didn't seem to get in the way of their bonding, which is almost always true with dogs, and it was after eleven o'clock when we called it quits, humans and dogs alike panting and tired. We all felt a little like teenagers out after curfew. And on the way home, the best thing of all happened: Scout peed curbside. I felt like turning a cartwheel.

After a fairly peaceful sleep, I woke up the next morning to a horrifying crime scene. Scout had chosen our red velvet living room couch as her sleeping spot. That was bad enough, but as I passed the couch I saw a little pile of broken glass and what looked like a knot of twisted brown plastic on one of the cushions. Upon inspection, I realized that this debris was the remains of Henry's replacement glasses, the ones he had ordered after Scout destroyed the first pair. They were his only pair of glasses; without them he was pretty much blind. The timing of this disaster couldn't have been worse: I knew that Henry was already about to explode under deadline pressure and frustration with Scout.

I walked into the bedroom to deliver the very bad news. I had rarely seen Henry lose his composure, but after he raced to the living room to survey the damage, I saw my fifty-five-year-old husband lying flat on the floor, pounding the wood, sobbing like a three-year-old. "I will never get my report done," Henry wailed. Scout crept into the adjacent room, seemingly ashamed to be the cause of such human misery.

I knew what my husband needed, besides replacement glasses, was a break from Scout. Ellen had told me that she often sent Charlie to spend the day at a day-care center for dogs in our neighborhood called Biscuits and Bath, so I got the phone number from her and immediately called the place. As long as Scout was six months old and we had proof of her vaccinations, she could come in for the day. Her age wasn't a problem, of course, and fortunately we had brought a copy of her health records with us to New York.

I had never thought about putting a dog in day care. In Buddy's time, when Henry and I both had to travel, either my sister or Jane Mayer usually took care of him. After we moved to Tribeca, when Buddy was being stubborn on his walks, I would sometimes tease him by telling him that I was going to leave him at the Wagging Tail, a day-care and dog-boarding place that we often passed on Greenwich Street. It had a plate-glass window that allowed you to watch the dogs, whose tails were rarely wagging. Most of the forlorn faces pressed near the glass looked worried, as if the dogs doubted they would ever be picked up and taken home.

But this was an emergency. Right after breakfast, I walked Scout over to Biscuits and Bath on Franklin Street. The chain—which combines unleashed (i.e., no cages) day care with various grooming services—has operated in New York City since 1990 and caters to working New Yorkers with unpredictable hours. Its motto is "Fun, Friends, and Freedom." Behind the reception area there are two large rooms, one for small dogs, the other for bigger ones. Both are padded in bright blue foam. Cheerful dog murals adorn the walls. The only problem for me was the fee, a hefty forty dollars a day. But in truth, I would have paid more so that Henry and I could both do our work that day, away from Scout.

Once inside the door, I decided that I might as well check out the fees for the grooming services. Surprisingly (to me anyway), they are not so different from the fees at human spas nearby: it costs twenty dollars to have dog nails clipped—about the cost of a Manhattan manicure—and sixty dollars for a bath and blow-dry. At those prices, I would stick to our home beautification regime of weekly baths, which Scout disliked but tolerated.

Welcome to New York, I thought, where there is a dog version of every kind of human service. At Pawtisserie, dog owners can drink coffee with their dogs and buy them frosted biscuits. In our neighborhood, there is a retired restaurateur who prepares freeze-dried meals just for dogs. To me, this anthropomorphized dog world is both fascinating and horrifying. I thought about Temple Grandin's descriptions of her dogs during her childhood and how they roamed freely in a pack throughout the day. Manhattan is as far away from that kind of life as one can imagine.

Happily, Fred Holmes, the manager of Biscuits and Bath, seemed like the nicest kind of person. Scout let him pet her right away and, of course, accepted the biscuit he offered. After signing a few papers, providing a copy of Scout's health records, and forking over my forty dollars, I handed Scout's leash to Fred. As I watched, Fred took her into the small dog room, where her friend Charlie and four other dogs were already playing. Feeling a tad apprehensive and guilty—we had never left Scout with strangers before—I headed for the subway to go to the *Times*.

I called Henry in midmorning and was greatly relieved to hear him sounding chipper. And there was good news, too: the replacement for his replacement glasses would be ready the next day. Henry offered to pick Scout up at Biscuits and Bath; later, he actually showed up a few hours early because he missed her.

By the time I arrived home, Scout was sound asleep. "It seemed like she had a great time," Henry said. "She just played and played." Henry had learned that the dog handlers always take their charges out a couple of times a day, and that Scout had relieved herself outside, not inside. He had also discovered that the rates are lower by the month. "I think I'm going to sign her up for the rest of September," Henry said. "It will give me the hours I need to finish the report." During those first few weeks in Manhattan, Biscuits and Bath was a lifesaver. Scout came to like the place so much that she would pull hard toward its front door the second we rounded Franklin Street.

Only later did I learn that we had almost certainly made a big mistake by not exposing Scout to Manhattan in her earliest weeks. When I consulted Dr. Katherine A. Houpt, the James Law Professor of Behavior Medicine at Cornell University College of Veterinary

Medicine, she told me that dogs, like children, learn most easily through early exposure to new experiences. Houpt said that it probably would have been less stressful for Scout to acclimate to all the New York sights and smells if she had made visits to our apartment during her first weeks with us. Young puppies, she explained, are open to just about everything, but an older puppy like Scout can find New York City awfully intimidating.

Luckily, though, Tribeca is an unusually dog-friendly neighborhood. True, it's full of trendy restaurants and expensive boutiques, but it is also filled with lots of young families, many of whom seem to own dogs. In our building, which has eight other lofts, there were three dogs for Scout to meet and potentially befriend. I had already spoken to the owner of a pair of dachshunds who lived on the floor above us, and she was excited about introducing Scout to her dogs.

There are also a number of dog runs within easy walking distance of our apartment. Though Scout was kept very busy at day care, Henry and I wanted to be sure that she got plenty of exercise in the mornings and after I returned from work, so we tried out several different dog parks along the river. Each had a slightly different character and clientele. At one near the boat basin at the World Financial Center, the human regulars were a tight group of friends who said "Good morning" to me and Scout but little else. "Is she a golden?" I would sometimes be asked. But it was hard for the two of us to break into this cliquish scene where almost everyone and their dogs already knew each other. Sometimes Scout would succeed in getting a dog to chase her, but within seconds a third dog would run over and lure Scout's newfound friend away. Once again Scout would be pushed out of the play, and soon she would give up trying to get other dogs to play with her.

This dog run is clean and has a beautiful view of the river, so we kept returning to it. Scout's favorite dog at this park was River, a tiny, five-pound Jack Russell terrier that was everyone's second-favorite dog after their own. As in any pack, there was also a cool crowd of bigger dogs; Scout would sometimes try to barge into their play, but she was usually rejected. Occasionally Scout found a big dog eager to wrestle with her, but just as often she would shy away from the other dogs and sit by my feet near the benches. She had learned her social cues from a small pack of country dogs that saw her every day, often in both the morning and afternoon. Now she was discovering that, with the exception of Charlie, making new city friends wasn't easy.

The virtue of dog runs is that they allow city pups to socialize and run around without a leash. But there are dangers, too. Sometimes dogs are unexpectedly aggressive: tails and ears are bitten, and every once in a while an owner will get hurt by a suddenly out-of-control dog. Because my accident left me a bit unsteady on my feet at times, I was particularly anxious about getting in the way of running dogs. Once we entered the dog park, I usually found a bench and took a seat.

I was also turned off by the snobbishness of some owners, which seemed to rub off on their dogs. Although our building is across the street from a middle-class housing development, the artists who once filled our neighborhood are increasingly being crowded out by richer types. When Scout and I entered a dog run, some of the people already gathered there would continue talking on their cell phones and fail to offer even a cursory greeting.

Five minutes from our apartment we found an antiseptically clean, shiny new dog run that bore every mark of urban planning, with tidy landscaping at both entrances. But for me the park had all the charm of a doctor's office, including owners who often stood or sat in stony silence. Because it's long and skinny, the run is excellent for chasing and retrieving balls, which Scout usually loved. But she had no interest in going there, because it was missing the one thing she wanted: friends.

Finally we discovered that a nicer bunch of people

and dogs frequented the smelliest and least scenic dog run in Tribeca, about six blocks from our door. Often strewn with garbage, it was more than a little funky, which was why Henry started calling it "the funky run." The run quickly became Scout's favorite; now, whenever we would walk outside, she would pull hard in its direction.

Located on the same block as the local elementary school, the funky run been there for decades. A plain, flat asphalt rectangle, it offers human visitors little more than some simple wooden shelters and two ancient park benches. Its big attraction for Scout was a large kiddie pool made of rigid plastic; when the weather was warm, she liked to splash around in the water. The other dogs—mainly mutts but also some other goldens—were much more eager to play with her than the dogs at the other parks we'd tried. When the two of us entered the run, a group of dogs almost always barked a welcome and ran over to greet Scout. At last, she had won acceptance in New York.

The owners visiting these dog runs are mainly people in our cohort, aging baby boomers with dogs—or ABBDs, as Henry and I call them and ourselves. We like many of them, but some are a lot more obsessed with their dogs than we are. They will have loud conversations about the quality of their dog's poop (loose stool is a challenging problem in the city) and debate whether tennis balls are safe for play (apparently, dogs can chew the felt covers off of them and choke). I imagine that most of these owners were equally fretful parents, and that they are now as anxious about their dogs as they used to be about their kids. But I tried not to be too hard on them that fall; after all, I sometimes worried that Henry and I were treating Scout more like a human child than a dog, and that we were becoming just as obsessive as the other ABBDs in our neighborhood.

One morning, during a visit to a dog run near the pier where we parked our car, I ran into Julie Salamon, a former colleague of mine at the *Wall Street Journal* who was writing a biography of the playwright Wendy Wasserstein. Once I started talking with Julie and her husband, Bill Abrams, their dog Maggie—a shepherd-chow-ridgeback mix with, as Julie said, "a little Elizabeth Taylor thrown in"—took an interest in Scout. It was almost as if my friendship with her owners certified Scout as a dog worthy of Maggie's attention.

Julie and Bill were in the same boat as Henry and me. Their last child was about to leave for college and, like us, they had decided to fill their empty nest with a new dog.

"You'd think we would both want the freedom," Bill said. "The truth is, I like having Maggie around. I believe that change is one secret to surviving middle age and an empty nest, and for us getting a dog is a really good change."

All four of us are part of the fastest-growing segment of dog owners, over-fifty empty nesters. Curious to learn more about our cohort, I spoke to Kenneth Budd, executive editor of AARP's magazine. Couples who replace children with dogs are a "definite phenomenon," Budd told me. "People who are empty nesters but ten years away from having grandchildren are saying it's time for a fur baby." He added that baby boomers in their fifties have the urge to "fill the void" for a number of reasons. One is the human need to nurture. Another is our generation's compulsion to stay fit, which matches up well with a puppy's need for exercise.

Julie, Bill, and I agreed that watching a group of dogs interact at a dog park and trying to figure out which dogs are "popular" and which are badly socialized or too aggressive is a fascinating way to pass the morning. We also enjoyed the irony that our dogs had helped socialize us, since here we were reconnecting after being out of touch for a number of years. Meanwhile, Bill regaled me with amusing stories about Maggie's first weeks of puppyhood, when he walked her all over downtown Manhattan. "Supermodels at Cipriani SoHo were suddenly interested in talking to me," Bill said, laughing. I knew exactly what he meant. Scout, too, was a magnet for conversations with strangers, and if I had been single and looking to date, she would have been a great ice-breaker.

By the time Henry met his October deadline, Scout was a kindergarten graduate and beginning to feel at ease in the city. We still spent weekends in Connecticut, but we were thrilled to have her with us in Manhattan during the week. And now that Henry had finished his big project, we no longer needed to send her to Biscuits and Bath every day, though she still spent a day or two a week there.

Henry loved having Scout's company while working in our apartment. For my part, the long walks with Scout in the morning and evening bracketed a pressured day, and they provided a much-needed spiritual antidote to the worries that come with the job of being responsible for the *Times*'s news report. No longer did I walk alone through the streets of lower Manhattan, second-guessing the choices I had made for

Scout with her kindergarten graduation medal

the next day's front page or replaying a tense confrontation with someone who had been the focus of a story and called the managing editor to complain. Although I always carried my cell phone in case the *Times*'s news desk needed to reach me, I felt almost total freedom from worry when I was outside walking Scout. But my delight in Scout went beyond the pure pleasure of companionship or the joyous greeting at the door that all dog owners receive. Watching her chase errant leaves in the city or dig at root vegetables in our garden in Connecticut, I noticed the different phases of fall in ways I hadn't the previous year. Even though I don't love winter, I couldn't wait until Scout experienced snow for the first time.

In late October, two months into Scout's city immersion, I found another urban treat for her. Near our loft is an unusual clinic and day-care center for dogs called Water 4 Dogs, which specializes in hydrotherapy for dogs with ailments or postsurgical problems, but also offers fun swims for healthy dogs for thirty dollars.

A trip to Water 4 Dogs would be a luxury for sure. But since it was now too cold for Scout to swim outside in Connecticut, I figured she must be missing the water terribly. When my children were young, I had often taken them swimming in the winter at our neighborhood YMCA, which had an affordable membership fee. Now I would have to pay more for Scout to swim than I ever had back then. But I was curious, so I called and reserved a place for her on a Tuesday evening.

The person I talked to on the phone told me that dogs could swim alone or with their owners, so when Henry, Scout, and I set off for Water 4 Dogs, I took my bathing suit. Knowing that Scout was used to swimming in backyard pools and the Long Island Sound, I anticipated that she might want company at this unfamiliar city pool.

When we arrived, there was only one other dog in the pool. (The manager told me that the maximum number of dogs allowed for the one-hour swims was four or five, a relief to hear since the prospect of swimming with a pool full of dogs seemed about as appetizing as wading into a baby pool full of diaper-free toddlers.) The water, kept at ninety degrees, felt like a warm bath.

I got in first, and Scout quickly followed me. Henry—who was delighted that I had volunteered to be the designated swimmer—offered to shoot some video. Scout swam in big circles and enjoyed using a ramp that allowed her to get in and out of the water easily. As well, the sides of the pool had rails on which she could climb and rest between laps. We swam for about half an hour and then availed ourselves of the pool's spalike amenities, including fluffy towels, nice shampoo, and hair dryers. There was a shower for me and hoses with hot and cold water for Scout.

While I showered and dried my hair, the staff gave Scout her own professional blow-dry, which she seemed to have mixed feelings about, since I could hear her barking in protest. The fee—about what I paid for guest privileges to swim at a nearby health club—was too high to make this part of our weekly schedule. But it was fun for a special treat.

At the *Times*, where there is a coterie of devoted dog owners, I learned about yet more special dog services in New York. One of the paper's business reporters told me about a palatial farm outside of Manhattan that offers daily or weekly stays for city dogs, along with pick-up and drop-off car service. (The cost is twenty-six dollars a day, but the transportation to and from the place costs a stiff ninety dollars on top of the daily charge.) Scout and I also checked out a hotel for dogs in SoHo, where there are $115-a-night suites, replete with little beds, turn-down service, and flat-screen TVs. Like so much else for the canine set in New York, this hotel is designed to appeal more to humans than to dogs.

Even so, I understand why so many of Manhattan's dog owners are inclined to pamper their pups. A lot of people work in an office and feel guilty about leaving their dogs alone in their apartments for hours on end, and also for depriving them of their natural longing to be outdoors. Understandably, city owners often worry that urban life is simply too confining for dogs.

Experts differ over whether this is true. Temple Grandin told me in an interview that she isn't a fan of raising and keeping dogs in the city, but she also said that pets are usually fine as long as they got enough exercise. "Besides love," she said, "exercise is by far the most important thing for dogs. If a dog gets enough exercise in the city and is loved by its owner, it can have a good life."

Karen Overall, another animal behaviorist, agreed that a dog owner's most important responsibility is spending time with the pet and giving it plenty of exercise. It is true, she said, that dogs who are cooped up for hours in cramped apartments can acquire behavioral problems and are sometimes prone to obesity. But she also said that many city dogs live happy lives. In fact, Dr. Overall—a professor of psychology and behavior in the Psychiatry Department of the School of Medicine at the University of Pennsylvania—splits her year between city and country, and she has owned dogs for years.

Dr. Overall went on to tell me a bit about her current dog, Maggie, an Australian shepherd who was bred to herd cattle but is perfectly happy in her small apartment in Philadelphia. In the summer, Maggie lives at Big Bend National Park in Texas, where Dr. Overall does research. Maggie loves spending part of the year in Texas, but she is basically happy in either place, as long as she is with her owner. "Whether it's swimming in the Rio Grande and flirting with desert foxes and coyotes, or going to class and defending me from muggers, she wants to be with me because we are a team." Companionship trumps location, Dr. Overall concluded.

At the *Times*, one of my younger colleagues, Gabe Dance, tortured himself over whether to bring his dog to New York after deciding to move here in 2005. The dog, named London, had followed Gabe everywhere, from his childhood home in Colorado to graduate school in North Carolina. Because of his responsibilities in the *Times*'s multimedia department, Gabe knew he would rarely be able to get home before 9 p.m. Right before London's designated moving date, Gabe made the decision he calls "the most painful of my life." He decided to leave London with his parents in Colorado, where she could play outside all day with their other two dogs. "I just thought it was the right decision," Gabe explained, but he misses London fiercely and visits her as often as he can.

I appreciated how hard it was for Gabe to be separated from London, in part because Scout sometimes stayed in Connecticut for extra days with Henry, and these separations were hard on me. When Henry didn't have to see clients in New York, he preferred to split the week between New York (Monday night through Thursday) and Connecticut (Thursday night through Monday). This meant Scout could still be part of the farm crowd in Connecticut and then return to the city and reclaim her place at the funky run, where she now had established friends.

By early November, Scout had been visiting Biscuits and Bath regularly for two months, and one day Fred Holmes sent her home with a report card. "She is where she needs to be," Fred wrote. "She is healthy, happy and interacts well with other dogs. That being said, Scout also has a strong personality and sometimes has more love than she knows what to do with and being a puppy this comes out as goofy, mischievous, silly behavior—all of which is encouraged."

She was, I was not surprised to learn from Fred, the class clown.

CHAPTER FIVE

Whether we were in New York or Connecticut, Scout's morning greeting usually came promptly at 6 a.m. when she arrived at our bedside, her big squeaky duck in her mouth. She often carried something in her mouth when she was excited, and in the mornings she brought the duck as an offering, an invitation for immediate play. Even then, two and a half years after the accident in Times Square, my leg was usually quite stiff first thing in the morning, so left to my own druthers I probably would have wanted to sleep a little later. But over the past few months Scout and I had developed a mutually agreeable morning routine.

I would first sit Indian-style on the bedroom floor

for a few minutes while Scout walked in circles around me, duck in mouth and braying with happiness. Then I would try to grab the duck, which, of course, I never managed to snatch away. Once I felt limber enough, I would haul myself up and chase her.

But one morning in November, when she was seven months old, Scout failed to appear on cue. It was a weekday morning in the city, and without my trusty alarm clock I overslept. At about eight o'clock, when Scout finally dragged herself into our bedroom, I could see immediately that something was wrong. Her eyes were glazed and she exhibited no trace of her usual morning playfulness.

A few minutes later, I had to pull her out for a walk when usually she was the one who pulled me. She also had no appetite. That afternoon, when she seemed no better, we decided to take her to the veterinarian near our house in Connecticut, where she had gotten her puppy shots.

The vet took an X-ray to make sure she didn't have some sort of intestinal blockage, and we were instructed to take her home and give her some Pepcid from the drugstore. But even after taking several of the acid-controller tablets, she was still out of sorts. I felt helpless and worried; her droopy gaze and listlessness made it apparent that she was ill, but of course she had no way to communicate what was wrong.

As with a sick infant, a dog's illness can be especially frustrating to diagnose. Whether in my role as a parent or a dog owner, I had never handled these sorts of medical problems very well. We had taken our children to the emergency room a few times with high fevers or after other mishaps; I recall with particular dismay the time Will got one of Cornelia's long crafting needles stuck in his foot. In these situations, I was always a nervous wreck while Henry remained admirably calm and reassuring. And whenever Buddy was ill and had to be taken to the vet, I was similarly agitated.

As soon as we got back to New York, I took Scout to see our vet in Tribeca, where Buddy had received uniformly good care. The vet ordered a blood test and examined a fecal specimen. The results came back with a double whammy of city and country ailments. Scout had giardia, a common parasite in Manhattan that she could have picked up from feces on the sidewalk or at Biscuits and Bath. She also tested positive for anaplasmosis, a tick-borne illness that she might have caught in our yard or at the farm. Our house in Connecticut is near Lyme, the ground zero for Lyme disease, which is also carried by ticks, and although Scout had been vaccinated for Lyme disease, the vaccine didn't protect her from anaplasmosis. Although we routinely checked Scout for ticks and tried to keep her nose off the ground on Manhattan sidewalks, it was impossible to be perfectly vigilant.

Our vet in Tribeca told me that neither of these infections is serious. But it's important, she said, to complete the full course of treatment, a three-week-long regimen of antibiotics. To ensure that Scout would take the medicine, she suggested we use Greenies, a soft dog treat, to envelop the pills.

Scout perked up considerably in the next few days. But because her infections were potentially contagious, we had to keep her away from other dogs while she was taking the antibiotics. Deprived of her dog pals, she was mopey and glum.

It was a relief to see her healthy again, but then one day, just after finishing her drug regimen, Scout was running to greet her friends at the farm when she suddenly let out a piercing yelp. I dashed over to her; she was breathing heavily and obviously in pain. Henry and I called our vet in Connecticut again and were told to take Scout to a twenty-four-hour emergency pet clinic near New Haven.

Upon arrival, we learned that the clinic's X-ray machine was broken, so we were sent to a second clinic. There, the doctors were unable to diagnose the problem, though one of the vets detected sensitivity in her back. After deciding to give Scout a painkiller and inject intravenous fluids to rehydrate her, the vets asked to keep her overnight for observation.

When we went to say good-bye to Scout before leaving, she was lying down in a cage with an IV needle attached to her right front leg, one area of which had been shaved. She looked terribly forlorn and vulnerable.

As we got into the car for the lonely ride home, Henry said, "Please don't assume the worst." He knew exactly what dark corner I was visiting in my mind. I was thinking about our ordeal with Dinah.

In 1995, three years after we got Buddy, Henry and I began thinking about getting a second dog to keep Buddy company. This idea came to us after my then-boss in the Washington bureau of the *Wall Street Journal*, Alan Murray, told me he wanted to get a puppy for his two young daughters. Intrigued by the notion of getting a Westie, Alan asked me for guidance. One thing led to another, and that summer I returned to the same breeder in Maryland from whom we had purchased Buddy and collected two females from a new litter. Carting home those two white puppies in our minivan, I told my children, then twelve and ten, that we would let Alan's girls, who had never had a dog, pick the puppy they wanted.

When we got home, we put the two little puppies in the yard, introduced them to Buddy, and then awaited the arrival of the Murrays. Meanwhile, unbeknownst to me, Will had fallen head over heels for the smaller of the two pups—apparently she had a vulnerable look that claimed his heart. When the Murrays arrived, the two girls couldn't decide which puppy they preferred, so Cornelia, looking out for her little brother, tried to steer them to the bigger pup. Naturally the Murray girls decided they wanted the smaller one, but at the moment of turnover Cornelia handed them the bigger puppy. Unaware of the switch, they accepted it happily. Will was immensely grateful for his sister's intervention, which Henry and I learned about only after the fact.

We named our new puppy Dinah, but we also gave her the nickname Tiny. She didn't grow as quickly as Buddy had, which began to worry me. In September, at about four months, her back legs began to tremble. A passerby watched her one afternoon that fall as she played in our yard. "Look at her back legs," he called over to me. "They wobble. You should have that checked out."

I called our wonderful vet, Dr. Kay Young, who had given Dinah her puppy shots but hadn't seen her since.

Tiny Dinah

Dr. Young looked concerned as she examined Dinah. She ordered tests and did further research. In particular, she wanted to rule out a rare neurological disease called globoid cell leukodystrophy—also known as Krabbe disease—that is specific to Westies and cairn terriers. She sent Dinah's tests to the University of Pennsylvania's School of Veterinary Medicine, one of the best in the country.

A week later, Dr. Young called me with a devastating diagnosis. Dinah did indeed have Krabbe disease. There is no cure, and most afflicted dogs die within a year. This disease also affects humans, and in infants it's often fatal before age two.

When I got home from work that night, I found it almost impossible to believe that the perky little pup licking my face was likely to be gone in a few months. After a flood of tears, I called the breeder and informed her about Dinah's disease—since both parents have to carry the Krabbe gene for it to be transmitted, I knew she would immediately stop breeding Dinah's parents. Happily, the Murrays' puppy, named Furry, did not exhibit any signs of the disease; as well, she had already been spayed, so there was no danger of her passing on the gene for Krabbe. As heartbreaking as this situation was, I was glad it was our misfortune and not the Murrays', whose little girls were over the moon about their first dog. After all, we were still blessed with healthy, wonderful Buddy.

Not long after receiving Dinah's diagnosis, I got a phone call from Dr. Mark Haskins, a professor at Penn's School of Veterinary Medicine. Dr. Haskins told me that having a dog with Krabbe would be extremely valuable to his research, because while some Westies and cairns carry the Krabbe gene, it's extremely rare for a living dog to have the actual disease. He also hoped we'd donate Dinah to the large animal colony at Penn's veterinary hospital complex and invited me to come for a visit.

The notion of giving Dinah up was even tougher for our family to absorb than the fact that we would soon be caring for a puppy who would suffer seizures, blindness, deafness, and loss of motor control. We wanted to give her our love, not give her away.

Nonetheless, right after the Thanksgiving break I traveled to Philadelphia to meet Dr. Haskins, a kindly man with a gray beard and mustache. The Penn veterinary facilities are impressive indeed. The animal colony has enough room for dogs to roam free, and there are treatment rooms with little gurneys, some with tiny stirrups, just like human ones but in miniature.

Then Dr. Haskins gave me a stack of newsletters to read. They contained accounts written by the parents of children with Krabbe, and most were accompanied by pictures. The stories documented how this disease ravaged families by robbing children of their early motor development and then causing death. Reading the newsletters was emotionally draining, but it also put our own family's plight in perspective. If Dinah could aid the research of this fatal disorder—if she could help researchers take even a tiny step toward finding treatment for these children—how could we say no?

I asked Dr. Haskins if we could strike a compromise: what if we kept Dinah at home but brought her to Penn, as frequently as he wanted, for testing and observation? He agreed and even said he would help with the commute. For the next eight months, we alternated: sometimes we drove Dinah to Penn; sometimes Dr. Haskins's students or aides drove down to Virginia to pick her up. Usually she returned home in a matter of days. Although some of the tests were painful, Dinah showed no overt signs of suffering, and the people at Penn treated her like a medical celebrity. She remained sweet and playful, a great companion to Buddy and to us.

Several months after the diagnosis, Dinah did lose her eyesight, but her quality of life was still pretty good when she marked her first year. Dr. Haskins was surprised by her relatively stable condition. But a few months later, Dinah's limbs began buckling beneath her, and she started having seizures. When the seizures grew frequent, I was forced to accept the sad fact that it was probably time to end her suffering. I called Dr. Haskins and made arrangements to make one last trip to Philadelphia.

Because Dinah's most valuable contribution to Dr. Haskins's research would come from an autopsy, she needed to be put to sleep at Penn's veterinary hospital. I cried while I drove, but I'd composed myself by the time Dinah and I arrived at the hospital. A group of young doctors came to collect Dinah, and Dr. Haskins sat beside me in the waiting room for more than an hour to comfort me after Dinah had received her lethal injection.

Surprisingly, Buddy did not seem particularly traumatized by the loss of his companion. We wondered if he sensed something was wrong with Dinah and whether it had interfered with the normal bonding between dogs. When I asked our vet, Dr. Young, about this, she said she thought that may have been the case. Either way, Buddy seemed to enjoy being the sole focus of our love and attention once again.

One lesson I took away from the experience with Dinah was that it's very important to have a vigilant vet. Another—which we've learned from our own experience and from talking to many friends who have nursed their dogs through cancer and other chronic illnesses—is that a sick dog is often especially loyal and lovable, and can bring the pack, dog and human, closer together.

While Scout was suffering through her season of ill health, I got back in touch with Dr. Haskins. He remembered Dinah well, not least because she was the oldest dog with Krabbe his team had ever seen. He reported that there had been some new developments in research and treatment of the disease, including a requirement in New York State that every newborn be tested and research conducted on cord blood transplantation. Unfortunately, though, there was still no cure. He wished me luck with Scout and tried to reassure me by saying that most dogs make it through puppyhood with no serious illnesses.

During those weeks when Scout was sick, I did my best to keep my misery to myself around most friends and colleagues. Although some people understand immediately how involved a person can be in caring for a dog, a lot of people just don't get it. If I spoke too honestly, some might think I was crazy to be so distraught over Scout's illness.

Partly to work through my anxiety, I consulted Dr.

Ann E. Hohenhaus, a specialist in oncology and internal medicine at the Animal Medical Center in New York. "A sick pet is scary just like a sick baby, because neither can communicate their illness verbally, and both rely on the adults in their life to recognize and respond to the illness," Dr. Hohenhaus said. "Kids and dogs are both so darn cute that we can hardly stand it when they feel bad, but people without kids or dogs aren't always sympathetic to our plight."

Dr. Hohenhaus told me that many owners feel distressed when their pets are sick, especially when the diagnosis is unclear. She also suggested that we think seriously about getting pet health insurance. When Henry and I began comparing various plans, we discovered that, as with insurance for humans, pet insurance programs are complex. Some are expensive, and it's hard to know for certain what kinds of illnesses and conditions will be covered. Most plans offer tiers of coverage, which grow in price depending on the breadth of coverage, the breed of pet, the location of the owner, and other factors. When comparing the cost of the plans offered by two leading companies, I found that monthly premiums ranged from twelve to forty-five dollars.

Fortunately, Henry and I could manage to pay this cost, whereas many pet owners, of course, cannot afford either pet health insurance or veterinary care for complex health problems. But given Dinah's illness and now this scary experience with Scout, we were both concerned about the possibility of incurring another big out-of-pocket puppy health expense. It didn't help that Scout was, in dog-training parlance, extremely food-motivated. While her chewing had abated somewhat, I worried that her occasionally successful sneak attacks on our laundry basket could result in her swallowing a sock or something else that could cause an intestinal blockage. I had a number of friends whose dogs had suffered through the surgeries that resulted from this sort of problem, so I knew how expensive a blockage could be.

I also had several painful memories of Buddy's health crises. When he was a pup, Buddy got into a box of chocolates that one of our children had carelessly left within reach. (Chocolate is potentially poisonous, especially for smaller dogs.) An expensive nighttime visit to the emergency clinic ensued, during which Buddy had to have his stomach pumped. Then, at midlife, Buddy developed terrible skin allergies, requiring tests and even biopsies, before a change in his diet brought the problem under control. In the end, what we spent on Buddy's health care—as well as on Dinah's more serious problems—likely exceeded the cost of insurance.

When Buddy was alive, however, I hadn't even known pet insurance was available. And although it is growing in popularity, only about 2 percent of dog owners buy insurance. About a dozen companies currently offer pet coverage, including VPI Pet Insurance, which has been offering policies since 1982, and Hartville Group, which has a licensing agreement with the ASPCA. With most policies, the dog owner picks the veterinarian, pays the bill for any health problem, and is reimbursed from the insurance company after deductibles are paid.

But like human insurance, pet insurance can be hard to get. Sometimes preexisting conditions are not covered, and older dogs with congenital ailments may be rejected for coverage altogether. Sarah Kershaw, a colleague of mine at the *Times*, experienced just that sort of difficulty. About a year ago, her dog, a young shih tzu named Sammy, started shaking, panting, and even biting the dog walker. After absorbing medical expenses of about $1,200, Sarah learned that Sammy had liver disease, one that made it impossible for him to metabolize regular dog food. Worse, the vet told Sarah that Sammy might need a $1,500 operation. Sarah didn't have pet insurance and set about trying to get it. Unfortunately, the company she approached rejected Sammy, saying his liver condition made him ineligible for coverage. "It was not a happy ending,"

Sarah said, "because he will be four in January, and if this liver disease doesn't shorten his life, that's another ten years at least of potential health problems with no insurance."

In the long run, insurance can not only save an owner money, it can also save a dog's life. During my conversation with Dr. Hohenhaus, she cited cases where dogs with insurance were treated successfully for health problems that otherwise might have been too expensive to solve. Recalling her work with several of these owners, Dr. Hohenhaus said, "We were able to make the decisions based on medicine, not on money." Dr. Hohenhaus is such a believer in pet insurance that she gave her two nieces, both dog owners, pet insurance policies for Christmas one year. Later, when one of the dogs needed surgery for bladder stones, Dr. Hohenhaus received an extra thanks for the gift.

After completing my research, I finally decided that we should get insurance for Scout. Henry agreed, and we ultimately purchased it through the American Kennel Club for about thirty dollars a month.

Henry and I were miserable after leaving Scout overnight at the animal hospital in New Haven. Despite the reassurances I'd been given by Dr. Haskins and others, I couldn't stop worrying. It's true that most puppies never get dangerously ill, but it's also true that most people don't get run over by trucks in Times Square. Nonetheless, this had happened to me, and I'd probably been a little paranoid about medical issues ever since. Henry was attuned to this tendency and knew that even though I had been remarkably healthy in recent years, any encounter with doctors made me extra jittery—and that extended to Scout and vets.

We arrived home that night at 2 a.m., exhausted but too upset to sleep. Later, Henry told me he kept thinking about our friend Clyde Campbell, who had gone to heroic lengths to save his golden retriever, Sunny, from cancer, only to lose her after a year of costly treatment.

At nine the next morning, we were hugely relieved when the vet called to say that Scout had had a good night and seemed stronger. He told us we could visit her later that day.

Scout was mad with happiness when the technicians at the animal hospital escorted her into the examination room to see us. We had brought a ball to entice her to play, and she chased after it and covered us in kisses. She still had the IV in her shaved right front leg, and she looked so vulnerable that I almost cried again. But the sensitivity in her back that the vet had detected the previous night was gone. After a consultation with the doctors, during which they admitted that they weren't sure what was wrong with Scout, we decided to take her home. We left the animal hospital with another course of antibiotics and what the doctors called an "open" diagnosis—as well as a bill for $2,000. The enormous relief we felt compensated for the staggering size of the bill.

As soon as Scout got home, she plopped on the dog bed near our couch and went to sleep. She spent the next day or two taking it easy, and then, on her third day home, she appeared in our room on cue at 6 a.m. The squeaking of her toy duck and, better yet, her joyous braying were the sweetest music we had heard in weeks.

CHAPTER SIX

By December, Scout had entered full-blown puppy adolescence. She was now eight months old, and at more than sixty pounds she was large enough to pull me in any direction. And if she stubbornly planted her rear end on the ground, there was no way I could budge her.

In puppy kindergarten, Diane Abbott had warned us that adolescence could set in as early as six months and that it could provoke epic tensions between dogs and their owners, just as it often does for moody teens and their parents. Earlier that fall, I had occasionally bumped into Diane in Connecticut, and more than once I told her about a recent episode of disobedience and then asked, "How will I know when Scout hits adolescence?" Diane, who usually offered expansive answers to my questions, would merely laugh and roll her eyes. "Don't worry," she'd say. "You'll know."

Most animal behaviorists agree that dog adolescence, like human adolescence, is a period of testing and turmoil during which a dog tries out different ways of proving independence from the pack. The first sign of change is often physical. Just as, years ago, I had noticed the pimples that suddenly appeared on Cornelia's forehead or the deepening of Will's voice, I marked the onset of Scout's adolescence from changes in her appearance. By the end of the summer she looked like a somewhat awkward cross between a puppy and an adult dog. Her snout had become longer, and the hair around her neck, just like Cyon's and Bunny's, had turned curly, reminding me of the frilly neck lace favored by Queen Elizabeth. But Scout was much skinnier than her two older friends, and her back legs still looked ungainly and too long for the rest of her. Looking her over one August morning at the farm, Clyde had said, "She's still filling out."

Over the past two or three months, her behavior had changed, too. Although she still shadowed me wherever I went and was always ready to play, in early fall she began showing an independent, even rebellious

Adolescent Scout playing with her friend Newton

streak. At the farm, she struck out on forbidden side paths, delighted when other dogs followed her into the brushy woods where we could not see them. She knew the location of a few hidden swimming holes, and she would often race off to find them while pretending not to hear me calling her back. (I would quickly stop shouting "Come, Scout," because calling a dog that refuses to come is pointless and only reinforces its recalcitrance.) After a cold dip, she'd saunter back to the pack, looking as though she were wearing black boots because her paws had been dirtied by the brackish water. Occasionally during our visits to the farm Henry and I would force her to walk with a leash to prevent her from wandering off, but her misery over losing her freedom and being kept from her friends was usually too much for either of us to bear. Once free, she would run right back into the prohibited zones.

One weekend toward the end of October I decided to take Scout on a long walk around our neighborhood in Connecticut—but this time I would keep her on her leash, and I vowed that I would correct her each time she pulled. An hour later, my forearm aching and my willpower sorely tested, I let her run free on the beach across from Marian and Howard Spiro's house. Scout was thrilled to be off the leash and had a marvelous time retrieving a stick that I kept throwing in the Sound. By then she was a very strong swimmer, and her boundless hunger for physical exercise never failed to amaze me.

As Scout and I played at the water's edge that afternoon, Henry was just a few houses away participating in one of his last Sunday lawn bowling games of the 2009 season. He caught sight of us down the beach and waved. When Scout spotted Henry, she took off like a rocket and moments later plowed right into the game and began chasing the lawn balls. Miraculously, she did not knock over any of the bowlers, most of whom were in their eighties and had been enjoying their usual round of cocktails during the game. Finally, Henry managed to grab Scout as she flew by. He waited for me to arrive with her leash and then helped me drag her to the car. On the way home, we felt as though we were retrieving a rowdy teenager who had badly misbehaved at a friend's house.

Manhattan, meanwhile, seemed to incite Scout to behave in a particularly headstrong manner. One weeknight when I took Scout for a walk by the river, we approached Locanda Verde, a posh Italian restaurant that had opened on our corner a few months earlier. Although it was fall, the weather was still warm, and the restaurant's outdoor tables were filled with customers. Henry and I had tried the restaurant soon after it opened, if only to sample its signature dish, a garlicky roast chicken that we could sometimes smell from our apartment four floors above.

As Scout and I walked past Locanda Verde's sidewalk tables that evening, I wasn't paying close attention to her. Suddenly I felt a wrenching tug on the leash, and in a flash Scout had jumped up on a table where two gentlemen were sharing a dish of the famous chicken. Though she failed to grab any of their entree, she did succeed in knocking over practically everything on their table. Once I regained control of her, I offered the men profuse apologies. In true New York fashion, they took the disruption in stride and even offered to give Scout a piece of chicken, which I politely refused as I led Scout away. She certainly didn't deserve a reward for the chicken lunge, which I suspected she had long been contemplating.

Despite her rebellious behavior, Scout was still intensely human-focused, much more so than Buddy had been. She wanted to be with us at all times and accompany us no matter where we were going. To prevent the possibility of being left behind, she would sprint into the back of our car at even the slightest hint that we were driving off somewhere.

With her keen sense of smell, she always knew where Henry and I were. At Marian Spiro's suggestion, we had played hide-and-seek with Scout when she was a small puppy, which taught her how to locate us whenever we were out of sight. (We never fooled her, no matter where we hid.) Now, even when exploring the deepest woods on the farm, she could always run and find us within a minute or two.

Much to our relief, her wanton puppy destructiveness had abated, but in the meantime she had acquired some less than charming new habits. She now took particular pleasure in digging deep holes in our yard, where she often buried her toys and the marrow bones she loved to chew. When younger, she had learned to retrieve and return balls and Frisbees; now, this harder-headed Scout would dash after a ball but refuse to return it. Instead, she would grab it tightly in her jaws and then run away, trying to trigger a game of chase, her favorite. Even the best treats, such as chicken livers, were often useless in the effort to persuade her to drop something she coveted and wanted to keep, no matter how persistently we bargained. She would simply bat those sultry eyelashes at me, as if to say, "Catch me if you can."

Besides being headstrong, adolescent dogs, like teenagers, are often obsessed with sex because of hormonal changes. One of my friends at the farm remarked that "female dogs can get quite flirty" after their first heat. Scout had been spayed at six months, which was part of our agreement with Donna Cutler, the breeder. But male dogs, and even some female ones, humped her anyway.

Scout's frequent declarations of independence were easier to handle in Connecticut because we had a yard and could visit the farm or the beach. But in Manhattan she was always on a leash when she was outdoors, and this led to power struggles almost every time we went for a walk. On the streets of Tribeca, she usually knew exactly where she wanted to go and showed little interest in being led in a different direction. When we passed Charlie's apartment building, if someone happened to be holding the front door open, Scout would pull me right in. If I wanted to walk by the river, she would invariably pull me toward the side street that led to a favorite dog run. And when I approached the local pet store where we bought her toys and treats, she would plant herself at the entrance and refuse to move, even if it was after closing time and the store was shuttered and dark.

By late fall, leashed walks had become an ordeal. Besides the annoyance and occasional aching shoulder, I worried that Scout's relentless pulling might somehow cause me to reinjure my leg, especially now that the sidewalks near the Hudson River were sometimes icy at night. My biggest fear, though, was that one night she might pull free of her leash altogether,

Scout on a leash in New York City *(James Estrin)*

race into the heavy traffic near the river, and get hit by a car.

Sometimes it seemed as if Scout had forgotten just about everything she learned in puppy manners class. My patience running out, I called Diane, who once again confirmed that Scout was simply displaying all the classic symptoms of puppy adolescence. "It can seem as if they never learned simple commands like Come or Sit," Diane said. But just as she had told me that I would know puppy adolescence when I saw it, Diane now reassured me that Scout would eventually outgrow these behaviors and that we would somehow survive.

Because adolescent dogs can forget what they learned as puppies, Diane urged us to go back to the basics of clicker training and once again reinforce Scout's positive behavior by clicking and then rewarding her. She also encouraged us to try one of several leashes that are designed to keep dogs under tighter control. At her suggestion, we bought a head harness called the Gentle Leader, which wrapped around Scout's snout and made it almost impossible for her to lunge ahead while we were walking. But Henry and I didn't like it, partly because it looked so much like a muzzle, but mainly because Scout seemed utterly miserable and resistant every time we attached it.

My frustration growing, I wondered if we had dismissed Cesar Millan's stricter training methods too quickly. Maybe we had made a mistake by not teaching Scout to view either Henry or me as the all-powerful alpha pack leader in our family unit. Maybe she would behave if I, like Cesar, demanded more dog obedience. Still, I hesitated to embrace Millan's tactics, because I knew that dogs could be damaged by the command-and-control approach. Even some of Millan's more gentle precepts, such as withholding affection until a dog is calm, seemed both harsh and hard to follow. Every time I saw Scout at the end of a stressful day, I wanted to greet her as enthusiastically as she did me, even if that meant that she sometimes jumped up on me and showered me with her kisses.

When Cornelia and Will were misbehaving adolescents, Henry and I had kept our cool and been relatively permissive. Our house in Virginia became a place for our children and their friends to hang out, and it remained so well into their teen years. This required that Henry and I be extremely vigilant about prohibiting alcohol, and we sometimes confiscated car keys and insisted that one or more of our kids' friends sleep over. Our approach during these years was straightforward: we tried to make our children and their friends feel safely supervised in a house where we applied fair and consistent rules.

But now, with adolescent Scout, we had fallen down on the job. When we were in a hurry to go outside, we would occasionally forget to bring the clicker or the treats that were Scout's rewards for behaving well. When she pulled on the leash, we wouldn't always correct her right away and pull her back to a stance parallel to ours before allowing her to resume walking forward. We knew that, especially during a dog's adolescence, consistency is vital to successful training. But it was easier to let her pull us forward, and too often we allowed her to have her way.

Just before Christmas, Henry and I decided that enough was enough: it was time to become more serious about mastering Diane's training methods. Taking bold action, Henry volunteered to fly out to California and serve as my eyes and ears at ClickerExpo, a series of well-attended clicker-training sessions led by Karen Pryor, the trainer who had introduced Diane to the positive reinforcement approach. Henry thought about bringing Scout with him—Pryor allowed dogs to attend the sessions with their owners—but that would have been too much of a production. So Scout and I stayed in

New York, eagerly awaiting the fruits of Henry's education.

Despite our exposure to Diane's remarkable skills and her endless enthusiasm for clicker training, we hadn't quite grasped the depth of zeal within what Henry came to call Clicker Culture. Its truest adherents regard the clicker method not only as an enlightened way to train dogs but also as a means to a better life. That's a lot to claim for the average dog owner, who just wants to achieve a reliable Sit and Stay and, occasionally, an obedient Come. But having observed a pattern of interaction between Diane and dogs that seemed almost magical, we were eager to know more.

The ClickerExpo took place at the Hyatt Regency hotel in Newport Beach, usually a place to play golf and sit in the sun, not train dogs. Over four hundred people attended, almost all of them pet professionals of one kind or another. Surprisingly, women outnumbered men by a ratio of about 20 to 1, which was consistent with a dramatic demographic shift in the animal-training world since the 1980s.

In California, you can tell a lot about a crowd by the cars in the parking lot. Henry noted that a sturdy gray SUV with personalized plates claiming DOG WIZ stood just a few spaces down from RUFF FUN. Next to LABRADOR was PAWWFCT, while GOODDOGU was parked not far from a stray equestrian, HOSNRDR.

The training sessions and workshops were due to be held in a number of plush conference rooms inside the hotel. A good number of the participants, Henry discovered, had attended a ClickerExpo before. At any given moment, between twenty and forty dogs were present, most of them from midsized breeds and all of them alert and well behaved. A few tiny dogs were rolled about in canine strollers, which were just catching on in Tribeca and rare in Connecticut.

Whether human or canine, all of the attendees were there because of Karen Pryor. A petite woman with sandy hair and an open, kindly face, Pryor had been a scientist and dolphin trainer in Hawaii earlier in life. She developed her theories about the use of positive reinforcement while working with dolphins; as she explained to those attending the expo, a dolphin can't be leashed, whacked, yelled at, or threatened. Since such behavior would cause a dolphin simply to swim away, a trainer has to use rewards to persuade it to deliver a desired performance.

In the 1930s, the pioneering behaviorist B. F. Skinner demonstrated that what he called *operant conditioning* could train a rat to get a food pellet by pressing a lever when a light came on in its cage, and to ignore the lever otherwise. Later, dolphin trainers discovered that captured dolphins were astonishingly quick to learn that certain actions earned a reward. So the underlying principles of clicker training had been established years before—in fact, they could be traced back to Pavlov's use of dinner bells to prompt dogs to salivate even before food was presented to them.

Pryor first made waves in the pet-training world in the mid-1980s when she published *Don't Shoot the Dog!: The New Art of Teaching and Training*, a book that popularized positive reinforcement as an antidote to the coercive, aversion-based training. In the bad old days, training too often relied on yelling at dogs, yanking their leashes and collars, and whacking them with rolled-up newspaper—not to mention using a range of dubious housebreaking practices. Pryor's approach was revolutionary, but for all its scientific underpinnings, her method appealed to many pet lovers because it was humane.

At the heart of Pryor's method is the consistent use of a clicker, which she employs as a tool for communicating a positive response to a particular behavior by a dog. As Pryor explained in her books and at the expo, a clicker's effectiveness goes well beyond the impact of spoken commands or praise. In her view, the technique—which she calls a technology—establishes new neural pathways in a dog's brain. She argues that clickers can prompt long chains of canine behavior that require split-second changes, such as those required in agility tests and other forms of competition.

During the expo's opening session, Pryor decried the popularity of Cesar Millan, asserting that he "legitimized the use of heavy punishment." But she also conceded that Millan's approach had recently become less coercive, and she seemed reluctant to appear too critical of his controversial methods. Then, after providing brief outlines of the expo's planned workshops, Pryor told the packed Hyatt ballroom, "We are changing civilization, starting in this room."

If that claim seemed overly ambitious, the expo did demonstrate that the clicker method had come a long way over the past couple of decades. In one workshop, a trainer of world-class female gymnasts showed how clickers—or sounds known as TAGs, for Teaching with Acoustical Guidance—helped teach young gymnasts how to land their heels precisely on the balance beam after executing a back flip. In that same session, several special education teachers discussed the use of TAGs to help autistic kids learn to socialize. And clickers were also catching on in zoos, where trainers taught large animals to lie down at the sound of a click. One zookeeper even trained a rhinoceros to recline for routine shots and nail trimming, thus avoiding the need for anesthetic darts.

Pryor's featured speaker at the expo was Victoria Stilwell, the star of Animal Planet's hit TV show *It's Me or the Dog*. Like her program, Stilwell's presentation was upbeat and amusing, and she incorporated a lot of entertaining video from the show. As well, she delivered her talk in an accent perfectly suited for the London stage, which is where she got her start.

As the name of her show suggests, Stilwell, like Millan, often parachutes into fairly desperate family situations. But unlike the pack leader, she never wrestles a dog in order to establish who's boss. The look in her eye, the tone of her voice, and the consistent lessons she teaches families and their dogs are what make her so effective—along with clickers and an avalanche of treats, of course. Perhaps the most revealing moment of her presentation came when she said that 80 percent of dog training depends on the owners and only 20 percent on the dogs; a hundred heads nodded as one.

Scout pined for Henry while he was away in California, and I often found her lying in her bed with one of his socks. When he arrived home, she was overjoyed. Once she calmed down, Henry presented me with some gifts from his trip, including books by Pryor and Stilwell and a new plastic clicker. Over dinner, Henry told me all about the trip, and it was immediately apparent that he had returned from California, as had many others before him, filled with the zeal of the newly converted. His eyes alight, his voice firm with conviction, he made a vow that very evening. "We are going back to Diane's basics," Henry said.

Soon after Henry's trip, I had the good fortune to meet Temple Grandin, the subject of a biographical film produced by HBO. I had asked to interview her before a screening of the film in Manhattan, though I worried that conversing with her might prove difficult because of her autism. But within minutes, Grandin put me at ease, and I was soon telling her tales about Scout's sudden transformation from gentle puppy to headstrong adolescent. For Grandin, whose autism gives her remarkable insights into how animals think and react, my story was familiar. But my talk with her meant something special to me in part because she had grown up with golden retrievers, including her beloved Andy, one of the dogs she wrote about in the book *Animals Make Us Human*.

Despite her flamboyant, bright blue satin shirt—which featured an embroidered image of cowboys riding horses—Grandin was understated, plainspoken, and authoritative. Because I thought highly of her books, including her autobiography, *Thinking in Pictures: And Other Reports from My Life with Autism*, I was predisposed to believe her theories about canine behavior and dog training. She, too, rejects many of Cesar Millan's methods as too punitive. But she does approve of some aspects of his approach to training, and she agrees with Millan that owners need to provide dogs with the equivalent of firm parenting, most especially by placing limits on their behavior.

When I told Grandin about my accident and the injury to my leg, she was quick to say that it was vital that we teach Scout to heel while walking on a leash. She also told me that even with the clicker and abundant treats, teaching a dog to walk on a loose leash is difficult. "What you have to understand is that walking on a leash is not their preferred state," she said. "Dogs need time to roam unleashed, either with humans or, better yet, with other dogs they know." I described our walks with Scout at the farm in Connecticut, which she thought sounded ideal. She told me she is not a fan of urban dog parks, although she conceded that taking a dog to a park is at least preferable to keeping it shut away by itself in an apartment all day.

I asked Grandin about the role that dogs played in her New England childhood, and she described how Andy would spend the day patrolling her neighborhood, exploring the nearby fields and woods, and participating in all the goings-on in town with the many other dogs who lived in her neighborhood. "That's not how we live anymore—dogs don't roam around unleashed," she said. "But the dogs preferred it that way."

She didn't view Scout's rebellious behavior as a serious problem. "It sounds like she is getting lots of love and exercise, which are the most important things. I think you should relax and just enjoy her." It was simple, commonsense advice, but because it came from Grandin I felt more resolved than ever to stick with Scout's training. I also felt new hope, because talking with her about goldens and seeing her light up at the memory of Andy reminded me of how much fun, love, and happiness Scout had brought into my life.

With winter came snow, and in Connecticut great drifts of it now stood right outside our doorstep. Just as I hoped she would, Scout adored playing in the snow almost as much as she liked splashing about in the water. But when she bounded outside I sometimes worried that her whiteness would make it difficult for me to keep her in sight. Years ago, after a very deep snowfall in Virginia, I became convinced that Buddy had become trapped under the snow. I called and called for him but saw no sign of his frisky little self. Soon I became frantic, certain that he would be smothered by the piles of snow. I ran to find Henry, who was taking a shower, and begged him to mount a search. Dutifully, Henry donned waterproof waders and boots and began trekking through the more than two feet of snow in our yard in search of Buddy—who, it turned out, had found a dry place in our greenhouse and was taking a peaceful nap. "You always think that Buddy is lost or in danger, and he never is," Henry complained afterward, with some justification. My tendency to blow up ordinary anxieties into life-threatening, worst-case scenarios annoyed Henry, and he often cited the Buddy Smothered in the Snow story to remind me how ridiculous I could be.

By now, though, Scout was too big to become lost in the snow, so I had little reason to worry. On snowy weekends, Scout and I usually met my friend Barbara Pearce and her Lab, Xena, at the farm. Xena was two weeks younger than Scout and about the same size, but she was much wilder. (Barbara used to take Xena running with her, but she had stopped because Xena pulled too much.) While Barbara and I chatted, Scout would lead Xena down the paths into the woods where we could no longer see them. Then, suddenly, they would dart back into our view, snow flying off their coats.

When they were small puppies, Xena was dominant; during their play, Xena would usually end up on top, sometimes with Scout's throat, or at least an ear, in her teeth. But now Scout gave as good as she got, and sometimes she pinned Xena to the ground. The shy puppy of a few months earlier was gone.

Also gone was the omnivorous eater. One cold morning, we put Scout's bowl of kibble and yogurt frosting down for her as usual. She wouldn't take a single bite. At dinner, she repeated the performance.

"Don't worry," Henry reassured me, "she won't starve."

Once again I was reminded of my children. As a teenager, Will had become a fussy eater. He would reject whatever dinner I made and cook a hot dog for himself. I worried that he would get nitrate poisoning, but like many adolescents he seemed to remain healthy and fit no matter what went into his stomach.

Reflecting on Scout's sudden disdain for the food she'd been eating all her life, I decided that she had become bored with the same bland diet. I could understand her reaction: being fed kibble with yogurt day in and day out might get a little tedious. I still yearned, of course, to return to my epicurean days of cooking a plat du jour for Buddy. But Henry was still insisting that we refrain from giving Scout human food at meal-times, using it only for high-value treats.

Unwilling to allow Scout to go without food, I went to our local pet shop with the notion of purchasing several "natural" brands of kibble to try out on her. They were far more expensive than the Pro Plan we usually bought at Petco, but I thought these so-called better brands might be worth a try. The store generously gave me several samples, so Henry and I decided to conduct a taste test. We put the samples in different bowls, labeled them, and then watched as Scout happily scarfed down all of them. To our discerning eyes, though, she seemed to favor one called California Natural, which claims to be grain-free and thus better for dogs with sensitivities to wheat or corn.

These "natural" kibbles had recently become all the rage, and even Petco planned to unveil a new premium line of "natural" kibble. At the very least, these brands make sense from a marketing point of view, since they can be priced more aggressively and appeal to upscale consumers who themselves prefer eating "natural" or "organic" foods. But some animal nutritionists I respected had expressed doubts about whether they offer real nutritional advantages.

Meanwhile, a number of dog owners had moved

beyond the arguments about which purchased foods are best. They passionately espoused cooking for their pups using some of the same foods—such as chicken, fish, sweet potatoes, and green vegetables—that humans eat. (For these owners, there are cookbooks full of dog-friendly recipes.) Scout even had a puppy friend named Newton, also a golden, who was fed only raw food. Henry and I were intrigued enough by the raw diet to give it a try with Scout, but when we purchased the recommended product—a tube of frozen brown matter that included beef lung in the list of ingredients—neither she nor we liked the looks of it.

In the end, the concoction that Scout found tastiest was one I designed myself, a special mixture of Pro Plan and California Natural, laced with a bit of meat and vegetables from our previous night's dinner. Soon Scout was eating again, I was cooking again, and Henry wasn't raising any objections. Everyone was happy.

Right after the new year, I had to go on a business trip to China, and Henry—who wanted to seize the opportunity to see the country for the first time—decided to come with me. This would be our first planned separation from Scout, and since we'd be away for a full week, we were nervous about leaving her. Fortunately, Will and his girlfriend, Lindsey, offered to dog-sit for Scout, in part because they were yearning to get a puppy of their own. I wondered whether they were really up to handling a puppy in full-bore adolescence, and naturally I worried that there might be some terrible mishap while we were away. During the workday, Will would be dropping Scout off at Biscuits and Bath; would he forget to pick her up in the evening? And if Lindsey, who was even smaller than I was, took Scout out for a walk, would Scout drag her into the gutter? I didn't share my fears with Henry, knowing that he would immediately roll out the Buddy Smothered in the Snow story.

The trip went off without a hitch, and while we were in Asia Will sent us several e-mails saying that Scout was fine. I didn't quite trust his cheery reports, though; I expected that upon our return we would hear a few horror stories. But after we walked in the door and basked in a deluge of kisses from Scout, Will and Lindsey assured me that Scout really had behaved extremely well.

The unexpected benefit of our time away was that it opened Will and Lindsey's eyes to the considerable responsibilities of owning a dog. "Cold reality set in the first morning," Will admitted. He worked in the music industry and was accustomed to staying up late at night and sleeping late in the morning. Lindsey, meanwhile, left for work by 8:30 a.m. and didn't have time to take Scout for a walk before heading out the door. But Scout had her habits and demands too, and at 6:00 each morning there she was, up and ready to play. During that long week with Scout, Will and Lindsey realized that at this point in their lives, their schedules were incompatible with dog ownership. "We don't want a dog less," Will told us, "but we better understand the limitations it puts on your life." Henry and I were glad he and Lindsey learned this lesson now, since too many people buy or adopt a dog on impulse, only to find out later that they can't care for their pet.

As for Scout, she seemed to have enjoyed her time with Will and Lindsey. While Henry and I unpacked, Lindsey proudly urged Scout to demonstrate some new tricks she had taught her, including how to stay in a down position and how to roll over. With Lindsey clicking away, Scout seemed thrilled to show off her newly acquired routines. No longer was she a wide-eyed new pup, but she was still wonderfully teachable and eager for new experiences.

Seeing our beautiful girl again after a week's absence gave Henry and me new confidence that we would indeed get through Scout's adolescence. We had survived Will's adolescence, after all, and now he was a loving and responsible adult. In the weeks and months ahead, we needed to reclaim the patience and grit that had made it possible for us to navigate our children's adolescent years and help them reach their full potential. We owed that to ourselves—and, more important, we owed it to Scout.

CHAPTER SEVEN

Now nine months old, Scout was the whitest golden retriever we had ever encountered—as Henry's sister put it, she was the color of a polar bear. Except for one precious soft spot on the top of her head, her coat was wiry. She was a bit stocky, too, with powerful legs and a solid middle. And her brown eyes and long lashes were still irresistible.

When Henry and I weighed her in January 2010, we were amazed to see that Scout tipped the scales at seventy pounds, ten pounds heavier than Donna Cutler had originally guessed she would weigh. She was close to her adult size, and when we took her for a winter outing to the farm in Connecticut or to the funky run in Manhattan, it was hard to believe that she had once been so tiny that Donna's nickname for her, Cindy Lou, invoked the smallest creature in Dr. Seuss's Whoville.

But though Scout looked all grown up, she was still in the early stages of adolescence, and suddenly she was gripped by a fear that wouldn't let go. She was scared of German shepherds—all German shepherds, even friends like Viggo.

Viggo, a large, one-year-old shepherd, belonged to our friend Lee Gibson, a warm woman with red hair who had become a big dog lover in her thirties. We often saw Lee and Viggo during our walks at the farm, and when Scout was a young pup she had happily played with Viggo. Now Scout responded very differently. On those winter mornings when Viggo didn't make an appearance at the farm, Scout jumped out of our car and ran ahead of me to greet the other dogs in the Breakfast Club, throwing snow off her fur as she galloped. But if Lee and Viggo were there, Scout stuck by my side, almost cowering. Since Scout was nearly as big as Viggo, I could not figure out why she was suddenly afraid of him.

It wasn't just Viggo. If a German shepherd entered the funky dog run in Tribeca, Scout would instantly become wary; instead of continuing to wrestle with her friends, she would lie underneath the bench where

Scout at nine months *(James Estrin)*

I was sitting. When I tossed a ball for her to retrieve, she would not run after it if a shepherd was nearby. Given the popularity of the breed—German shepherds are sturdy working dogs, famous for their work with police forces and as guide dogs for the blind—we ran into them pretty frequently. They were beautiful, intelligent, extremely loyal dogs.

I vividly remembered our first encounter with Lee and Viggo at the farm the previous summer. On a beautiful Sunday morning, I saw Lee working alone with Viggo in a field, teaching him how to retrieve and then relinquish his ball. Since I was trying to get Scout to master the same skill, Scout and I watched them for a while. Lee—who was clearly an expert trainer—used a clicker to mark those times when Viggo brought the ball back and dropped it at her feet.

After about half an hour, Lee introduced herself and suggested that we let the dogs play together. As Viggo and Scout happily chased each other around the field, Lee explained that Viggo would not always be hers. He had been placed with her when he was just eight weeks old, she told me, and for the first year of Viggo's life she would be training him to be a guide dog for the blind. In early 2009, she had volunteered at a nonprofit organization called Fidelco, which had matched her with Viggo. The organization, based in Bloomfield, Connecticut, has been training guide dogs for the blind since the 1960s, and at the time Lee volunteered, Fidelco had more than a hundred dogs in foster homes around Connecticut.

There were ten puppies in Viggo's Fidelco litter, all of whom were given names that began with *V*. Fidelco's standards are extremely demanding: not all of the puppies who begin the program ultimately graduate and are matched with a blind person. If Viggo got through the first stage of training, which would end soon after he was fifteen months old, he would return to Fidelco for intensive training. Then, if he passed the final hurdles, he would be placed with a blind person. If Viggo flunked out at any stage of his training, Lee would be given the option to keep him.

Fidelco's rules are strict and Lee added some of her own. She gave Viggo several hours of exercise a day, fed him a special raw diet, and kept him in a crate most of the time he was inside her house. Once a week, Lee and Viggo were required to attend a group class with the other pups in the *V* class. Besides exercise, the most important thing for Viggo to learn was proper socialization with people and other dogs. The farm, with its pack of playful dogs, was a perfect testing ground.

Not long after Lee and I first met, Lee noticed that Viggo would occasionally bully Scout. Lee knew Viggo's every move; she also knew that German shepherds as a breed are protective. Early on she had perceived that Viggo was *dog reactive*, a term she used to describe his intense reaction to unfamiliar dogs. If Viggo saw a dog he didn't know in the distance, his hackles (the hair on the back of his neck) would rise and his ears would prick up. As Lee knew well, these are signs of watchfulness and possible aggression—or, as she put it, "a display to create a barrier."

Viggo's response to strange dogs—Scout included—was hardly unusual, especially for an adolescent male. But Scout was too young to read Viggo's body language, and she did not always respect his barrier. She treated Viggo like everyone else, dog and human, rushing to greet him too impulsively. When she did, Viggo would indicate his displeasure by thrusting himself into Scout's physical space and staring her down. This hostile behavior wasn't at all difficult for Scout to interpret, and long before I did, Lee saw that Viggo's bullying scared Scout quite badly.

Lee worried about Viggo's aggressiveness because he had to be consistently calm and focused in order to be accepted into formal guide-dog training. Viggo could not pull on his leash, as Scout routinely did, whenever anything of interest—a squirrel or a blowing leaf—appeared in his field of vision. After all, a sudden pull could potentially be calamitous for a blind person. Viggo also couldn't act up around new people or around new dogs. Lee knew that, by nature, Viggo was both protective and sweet-tempered, which is why she worried when he suddenly became uncharacteristically aggressive.

Lee was especially bothered, she told me later, by an incident at the farm that had happened before we met her. Viggo had run over to a gentle Lab, stolen the stick in its mouth, and then nipped the Lab. That experience made Lee particularly vigilant when Viggo encountered other dogs. Often, she preferred to walk him alone, on the leash, at a state park a few miles away. But Viggo needed to be almost perfectly socialized if he was going to succeed as a guide dog, so Lee continued to bring him to the farm and monitor his behavior around Scout and the other dogs.

I didn't understand that Viggo was bullying Scout until weeks after their first antagonistic encounters first began occurring. Even then, it took me a while longer to associate Scout's discomfort around all German shepherds with Viggo. I, like Scout, was only just beginning to learn the skill of interpreting dogs' social cues. Because Buddy had spent most of his time alone, patrolling our yard, I had missed out on the chance to learn about dog manners and socialization. Now, raising Scout and witnessing her behavior in various social situations—including Marian's back-yard, the farm, Biscuits and Bath, and the funky dog run—I was learning a lot about how dogs interact.

Meanwhile, Scout's fear of German shepherds continued to grow. In the city, she insisted on performing a thorough inspection of a dog park before entering it. She would stand for a minute or two at the fence enclosing the run, casing the joint to make sure that no shepherds lurked inside. If one appeared with its owner while we were inside the run, she would stop playing and come lie down under my legs. On the outside, she was Scout, a beautiful, nearly full-grown dog. On the inside, though, she was sometimes still Cindy Lou, a born worrier and the littlest resident of Whoville.

All dogs live with some measure of fear, and because puppies are inexperienced in the ways of the canine world, they tend to be especially susceptible to a range of anxieties. In this way, too, they are not unlike children.

Anxiety, whether in dogs or humans, is complicated and interesting, and perhaps because I grew up among a collection of lovable neurotics in New York City, I have long been fascinated by my family's various phobias. My sister Jane, for instance, developed a deep-seated fear of the Babar books when she was a little girl. Where previously the books had been her favorite read-aloud stories, Jane suddenly became fearful of the illustrations of a minor character, the wizened and white-haired Old Lady. Although our mother explained that the Old Lady was a good character who often came to Babar's rescue, my sister was nonetheless petrified of her prune face and long black coat. But since she couldn't bear the thought of putting the books away altogether, Jane instructed Mom to continue reading about Babar's adventures but skip the pages involving the Old Lady. Not only did this on-the-fly editing prove to be a successful workaround; it also may have planted the seed of a future career, since Jane ultimately became a successful children's book author and editor.

But Jane was hardly alone, and I had my own battles with fear when I was a girl. In the third grade, I was mercilessly bullied by a clique of alpha girls in my class. Although only nine years old, they hatched a sophisticated plan for torturing me. Pretending to be twice their age, they called Saks Fifth Avenue and an expensive butcher shop in Manhattan with instructions to deliver a number of items—including fancy clothing and several pounds of extremely costly cuts of meat—to my family's apartment. When my mother started receiving packages addressed to me that she hadn't ordered, she knew something was wrong. And when a succession of little girls phoned our house, asked for me, and then collapsed into giggles before hanging up, she quickly figured out that some of my classmates were playing a mean practical joke at my expense.

It didn't help that the miscreants were ultimately identified, because suddenly I did not want to go to school. I also developed an irrational fear that I was going to be "left back," or not promoted to the next grade, which had happened to a classmate the year before. The mean girls were making me feel like a loser, both socially and intellectually, and though they soon moved to another target, I couldn't keep my eyes off them during recess and lunch, terrified that they might strike again.

Years later, my own children battled phobias of their own. When Will was in first grade, he had trouble adjusting to a new school in Virginia. Though Will and I were close, he wasn't able to admit to me that he was very anxious about this change. Each morning, when I walked Cornelia and Will to the bus stop, Will seemed eager to go to school. But once there he refused to take off his jean jacket. While the other pupils removed their coats and put them in their cubbies, Will insisted on wearing his jacket throughout the day. His teacher Mrs. Larson knew a lot about children and wisely interpreted this as a sign that Will wasn't happy and wanted to be prepared in case he decided to make a sudden getaway.

That September, when I came to her classroom for the ritual parent-teacher meeting, Mrs. Larson mentioned her concern about Will's refusal to take off his jacket. This did not sound like my boy, who had always been so easygoing. After several nights of casual chatting right before he would nod off in bed, I gently broached the topic of his jacket. Out tumbled all his worries: Did the kids in his new class like him? Would he ever have friends to eat with in the lunchroom? Were his sneakers cool enough? I reassured Will that it was normal to feel scared in a new school and that he would make lots of friends, just as he always had. (I also silently reassured myself that when winter arrived his heavier parka would be too warm to wear inside.) Sure enough, Will's fears gradually eased, and a few weeks later Mrs. Larson gave me a call to say that his jacket had come off and his troubles seemed to be over.

In all of these cases, time and a little cleverness were the best antidotes, and so it was with Scout's shepherd phobia. At the funky run, plenty of dogs of other breeds raced to greet Scout when she appeared in the morning. Often she was so busy running or wrestling with one dog or another that she didn't notice when a German shepherd visited the park.

One day, a ten-year-old shepherd named Daisy entered the funky run and soon joined the fray. A few minutes later, she bowed before Scout, inviting her to play. I expected Scout to run in my direction and try to hide, but this time she didn't. The two dogs wrestled, and when Daisy pinned Scout to the ground, Scout made her mock-ferocious wolfie face. They continued playing happily for the next ten minutes, until it was time for us to go.

As we left the run, I took Daisy's owner aside and asked if she would be willing to coordinate her visits to the funky run with ours for a week or two. She graciously agreed, and the next few times Scout encountered Daisy she was always happy to play with her.

Scout's acceptance of Daisy as a playmate proved to be a breakthrough. At the farm, she was no longer intimidated by Viggo. Though they didn't engage each other in play, Viggo stopped bullying her, and Scout stopped cowering at my side whenever he was around. Now, she would rush to her friends even if he was present.

Then, suddenly, Viggo was gone. In late January, a month before Lee was due to deliver Viggo to Fidelco for his final training, Lee's partner, Deb, badly broke her ankle. Lee—who also had a full-time job—could not possibly take care of Deb, give Viggo his two hours of exercise, and go to work every day. Fortunately, Fidelco allowed her to return Viggo a bit early.

Before driving Viggo to Bloomfield, Lee took him on one last walk at the farm. The day was cold, and the only other dogs there were two rambunctious golden-doodles, Ikey and Kaboo. Lee watched as Viggo played with the two dogs in a light, easy way, even sharing his beloved Chuckit ball with them. "I was so proud of him," Lee told me later. It was a testament to her patient training that Viggo had turned out to be a good, social boy after all.

Months after Lee said good-bye to Viggo, I asked her about that last day, but she still had trouble talking about it. At first, she brushed past the subject, but then she admitted that it had been very painful. She wanted Viggo to have his toys with him, but packing them up had been terribly hard. Their parting had been upsetting, too, in part because after arriving at Fidelco she had helped lure Viggo into a crate, one that she thought was too small. And the drive home was simply awful. A couple of hours after our conversation,

Viggo just before returning to Fidelco *(Lee Gibson)*

she sent me an e-mail in which she confessed, "I was too embarrassed to admit that I sobbed on the ride back from Fidelco. Now you are the third person who knows that—the other two are my mom and Deb."

Reflecting on how attached I was to Scout, I found it inconceivable that anyone could give up a dog after pouring so much love and effort into training him or her. But dogs, like people, are happiest when they have a job to do, and Lee was very invested in helping Viggo achieve his purpose in life, which was to be a superb guide dog. However difficult it was to let him go, she was comforted by the knowledge that Viggo might soon be providing essential aid to a blind person.

Now that our pup's former nemesis had a serious job, I found myself wondering about Scout's purpose in life. Her current work—to get fully trained and stop pulling on her leash—seemed so trivial compared to what Viggo was doing. But Scout's job, I realized, was hard in its own way. She was struggling to grow up, to make the transition from a wantonly destructive, overenthusiastic puppy to a law-abiding, loyal, and happy dog. Like all major transitions, it wasn't easy.

Part of growing up involved learning new skills. In the front hall of our apartment in New York, which we called "Scout's school," we practiced all of her commands—Sit, Stay, Lie down, and the rest—but we also taught her new tricks like shaking hands with her paw and finding some of her toys by name, like Ball. We used the clicker to compliment her when these moves were well done, and we augmented the clicks with plenty of hugs and pats. She lapped up our attention and practically glowed with pride. Equally important, she craved to learn more.

But Scout was still a puppy, and sometimes she was destructive or just plain naughty. At the farm, she would forget herself and lead other dogs down forbidden paths. More worrisome, she continued to pull on her leash despite our best efforts to train her not to. By February she weighed seventy-five pounds, and now she could pull me right into the gutter, which she too often did if she spied a discarded McDonald's bag or some other irresistible temptation. In fact, just before Henry and I had left on our trip to China, Scout pulled me down and dragged me a few feet along the icy walk by the Hudson River. My lower back hurt enough that I was sure the long plane ride to Beijing would be ruinous; I was so concerned, in fact, that I even kept the news of this disaster from Henry. To my relief, my back was sore but not injured, but the experience delivered a sobering message. Scout was now so strong that she was capable of causing me serious physical harm. And given the residual effects of my accident, I couldn't help but worry about the damage that might occur the next time she pulled me to the pavement.

Far more often, though, I took pleasure in watching Scout behave like a typical adolescent. At my sister's house one day, Scout found a closet full of children's paraphernalia, most of it related to a series of books my sister had written about a character called Fancy Nancy. Among other things stowed in the closet was a little white stuffed dog named Frenchie. One afternoon, Scout broke in and stole her. My sister took the toy and returned it to the closet. On our very next visit, Scout stuck her head in my sister's fireplace and was instantly covered in black soot. Then she made a beeline for the closet and stole Frenchie again. When my sister saw that Frenchie, after being covered with Scout kisses, had become a little gray stuffed dog, she gave up and told Scout she could keep Frenchie for good. Laughing, she said, "I guess you want a baby now that you're big." Scout, seeming to understand that she had won her coveted toy, wagged her tail and kept her sooty jaws firmly clamped on Frenchie's hindquarters.

CHAPTER EIGHT

Not long after Henry and I returned from our trip to China, we decided that we had to do something about Scout's pulling. Even when I carried a sack of her favorite treats and gave her constant rewards for walking parallel to me on a loose leash, she frequently darted sideways or lunged forward at unpredictable moments. Now I had a phobia of my own: I worried that every walk to the funky dog run could end in calamity, with me sprawled on the icy sidewalk or, worse, with both of us lying in the street facing oncoming traffic.

In our use of positive reinforcement to train Scout on her leash, we employed a range of tools and techniques. We continued to use our clicker, which often but not always proved effective. We regularly dipped into the ever-present treat bag, which was stocked with enough meaty, moist, and delectable tidbits to provision a small expedition down the Amazon. We also tried attaching Scout's leash to a harness instead of to her collar, but although this relieved some of the strain on her neck, it did nothing to diminish her power to pull either of us along. Too often it felt like Scout was walking us, not the other way around.

Henry and I were convinced that in the right setting and with enough time and patience, the positive approach to loose-leash training could be highly effective. Neither of us had forgotten Diane Abbott's instruction to reward Scout every time she appeared at our sides in the heel position, and we did our best to be consistent about doing so. But when I was trying to hurry across a busy avenue in front of a flotilla of racing cabs, I could spare little time to entice Scout to forge on or follow my lead.

Scout did her best as well. She learned to sit at red lights when instructed, and then, on the command Let's go, to quickly cross the street. But though she was reasonably well behaved in traffic, whenever we approached the block leading to the funky dog run, she could not control herself. Every morning, the two of us presented the same absurd spectacle: as we approached the run, there was Scout running in front and me trailing behind, holding on for dear life. I felt like I was waterskiing—or, on snowy days, ice-skiing—behind a big golden boat.

Of particular concern was Scout's habit of pulling my arms from their very sockets at the sight of another dog. And there were dogs everywhere: in our building, on the street, walking along the river. Scout was curious about each dog we encountered, whether known to us or not, but if she saw a dog with whom she was especially friendly she would pull to kingdom come. One day that February I realized that Scout, at ten months old, weighed only forty pounds less than I did. No wonder her pulling frightened me so much.

I called Diane Abbott yet again, and she urged us to give the Gentle Leader one more try. But Scout simply wouldn't walk with it on; instead, she would plop down on the narrow and very busy sidewalk in front of our building. Since we live only a few paces from a gigantic apartment building and the downtown offices of Citigroup, our sidewalk is a human highway day and night, so lying down on it is not advised.

After I told Diane that the Gentle Leader wasn't working, she had another idea. Whenever Scout pulled, Diane said, I should stand without moving on the sidewalk. Then I was to divert Scout with a noise, either the clicker or another sound, and pull her back toward me. When she returned to my side, I was to turn and walk with her in the opposite direction for a few paces. Then I should command her to sit and give her a treat, after which I was to turn again and resume walking in the desired direction. At first I was optimistic about this strategy, but I quickly realized that following it required that I budget at least an hour to get anywhere because of Scout's persistent pulling.

More frustrated than ever, I spoke to Lee Gibson, who through Scout's first winter became almost as invested in Scout's training as I was. Lee loaned me a training manual called *My Dog Pulls: What Do I Do?* which was written by Turid Rugaas, a well-known dog trainer from Norway. Rugaas's book, replete with diagrams illustrating the preferred method of correcting a dog that pulls, confirmed Diane's basic principles of stopping, changing direction, and offering a treat before proceeding. But the approach described in the book only underscored how laborious a process this antipulling regimen could be.

As much as I would have liked to follow their advice, both Diane Abbott and Turid Rugaas assumed unlimited time for dog walks and a relatively calm environment in which to take them. But the realities of my life in Manhattan called for other means and methods. I needed time in the morning to read the full *Times* news report, master what the competition had published, and then take the subway to work. All this came on top of making sure that Scout had her walk as well as enough exercise and playtime. If I dutifully followed the Rugaas regimen and was constantly stopping to correct Scout's pulling, I would be hopelessly off schedule. And, frankly, dog owners like Diane Abbott and Lee Gibson were a lot more patient than I was. After weeks and weeks of working to get Scout to stop pulling, I began longing for a surefire cure.

The day of reckoning came when Scout encountered the two dachshunds that lived in our building. They and their owner were standing on a corner across Greenwich Street; when we arrived at the opposite corner, our light for crossing was red. As usual, I commanded Scout to sit while we waited for the light to change. But when the two dachshunds saw Scout and began barking at her, Scout bolted into the street, pulling me behind her. We were both nearly hit by a taxi, which screeched to a halt.

Our close call left me shaken and miserable: Scout could have been killed and I could have been run over again. This time, I didn't keep the incident secret from Henry, and when I told him about it he immediately agreed that we had to take more drastic measures.

That evening I happened to be having dinner with Sam Sifton, the *Times* restaurant critic. One of the perks of my job is occasionally accompanying Sam on visits to a restaurant he plans to review. That night we ate at Maialino, a new Roman-style trattoria that had recently been opened by Danny Meyer, one of the city's best restaurateurs.

Sam, a fellow dog lover, often asked about Scout, and he had particularly enjoyed the story of Scout's petty thievery at Locanda Verde. (After hearing my tale of woe, Sam commented, "At least she has good taste. That chicken is sensational.") Mere minutes after arriving at Maialino, I told him about my harrowing experience on Greenwich Street earlier in the day.

Sam immediately understood the seriousness of my problem. "You need to call in the heavy artillery, pal," he told me sternly. "You need CujoCop." He then handed me a business card for a dog trainer and New York City police officer who had trained bomb-sniffing dogs after 9/11.

Noting that CujoCop's card had an image of a German shepherd on it, I told Sam about Scout's aversion to the breed. "It doesn't matter," Sam said. "Cujo can train any dog and any breed. I know, because Joe—

our huge and very ill-behaved mutt—became the perfect dog after an hour with Cujo."

Sam then told me the story of how Cujo had come to the rescue not long after Sam and his wife, Tina, adopted Joe from an animal shelter in Linden, New Jersey. Claire, their younger daughter, "found" him on Petfinder.com, and though the director of the shelter told Sam that Joe was already spoken for, the Siftons decided to drive out to the shelter just to meet him. Joe—who was then two years old and weighed seventy-five pounds—was gentle and calm, and he sniffed at the two girls affectionately. Claire's instinct that he would be a sweetheart seemed correct.

Barely an hour after the Siftons returned to their home in Brooklyn, they got a call from the shelter. Joe was suddenly available again. "It didn't work out," a worker at the shelter told Sam. The man who had the first claim on Joe owned another dog, and when the two dogs were introduced tempers had flared. That same day, the Siftons drove back to New Jersey to collect Joe.

As advertised, Joe was a big, sweet, Lab-related mutt. But he also displayed some wildness: he had a tendency to nip the kids during play and to run hard at Sam or Tina. Sometimes he would jump up as if to bite them, his paws tearing at a loose pant leg or sleeve. Understandably, everyone in the Sifton family found Joe's occasional bad behavior frightening.

The final straw came when Joe attacked a couple of other dogs in the park and then bit a neighbor whom he perceived as a threat. "It was terrifying," Sam said. "We thought we'd have to get rid of him." Tina called the shelter to ask what to do. Someone at the shelter told her they occasionally worked with a trainer named Chris Velez, whose nickname was CujoCop. He'd know what to do, the person at the shelter said.

As it happened, Chris was stationed in the Siftons' Brooklyn precinct. Sam and Tina immediately arranged for Chris to make a home visit, which would involve a one-hour consultation and training session. When Chris arrived, he greeted Joe and then asked Sam and Tina a number of questions. While they talked, Joe sniffed Chris a few times before lying down at his feet. About half an hour later, Chris suggested taking Joe for a walk.

"Incidentally," Chris said as they made for the door, "you have a great dog. There is absolutely nothing wrong with him. You may have to change your behavior more than he will. He's a good guy."

Over the next few minutes, Chris taught Sam a completely new way to walk Joe. His approach was definitely pack-leaderish, like Cesar Millan's. "You can give him treats and rewards," Chris told Sam. "But someday you're not going to have treats or rewards in your pocket, and then you're gonna be in trouble."

Chris also stressed the need for Joe to have a job: a walk was about doing his business (defecating and peeing), not taking a leisurely stroll. There was to be no stopping to mark trees or greet other dogs. "We walk—that's the job," Chris instructed Sam. Only when Joe was thoroughly exercised and tired would he be released from his job.

Chris spent most of the session training Sam, not Joe. After Chris's initial visit, the Siftons scheduled a few follow-up consultations, and Sam sometimes called Chris with questions or problems. But from that first hour on, Joe's behavior changed. By following Chris's regimen, Sam said, they had brought out the best in Joe, and there had been no alarming incidents in more than a year. "Joe's a happy member of our household now," Sam reported. "That would never have happened without Chris."

As Sam told me the story of how CujoCop had worked wonders with Joe, including stopping his leash pulling, I became convinced that it was time to bring a tougher brand of trainer into our lives. Scout had learned her basic puppy manners in Diane Abbott's class. She had mastered a number of our commands and for the most part responded well to them. Henry and I, meanwhile, had clicked and treated her beyond all reason. Fundamentally, Scout was a good dog who tried very hard to please—except when she was on her leash. So after months of using positive reinforcement to train her to stop pulling, it was time to take a harder line. I would probably never become the calm, assertive pack leader extolled by Cesar Millan, but maybe Chris Velez could get me closer to that ideal.

I called Chris the next morning and spoke to his wife, Darcie. She was sure Chris would want to help with Scout's pulling, but there was a practical problem: Chris was finishing a tour in Iraq in the Army Reserves and wouldn't be back for several weeks. Darcie promised that Scout would be first on Chris's dance card when he returned.

True to his wife's promise, Chris called shortly after he arrived back in the United States. He could fit in an appointment one morning before he returned to work on the police force. Henry and I both arranged our schedules so that we could be there for his introduction to Scout.

Chris, a muscular, balding man with a wide smile, had been a police officer and detective for twenty years. Since 1995, he has trained search-and-rescue dogs for the New York Police Department. He has also long served as a corporal in the U.S. Army Reserves, and in Iraq he has trained dogs to search for explosives. When he came to our apartment that morning, he brought a brochure about his services that included a list of problems that he could mitigate or correct. When I scanned the list, there it was, just what we were looking for: "pulling on leash."

Like many New York cops, Chris has a genial but business-like manner that suggests both a high degree of competence and a quiet confidence that he has seen it all before. His dog-training equipment consists of a leather leash and metal slip collar, sometimes known as a choke chain or choke collar. After a few minutes of preliminary conversation, he explained how to position the slip collar. "It won't choke or hurt her if you use it correctly," Chris promised, seeing my frown at the notion of putting a chain around my puppy's neck. But I had resolved to get tougher—maybe the slip collar would help, I rationalized. Soon, Chris, Scout, Henry, and I all headed outside to test the Cujo magic on the street.

Dog trainers are close observers of people, too, and Chris seemed to sense our anxiety about Scout's difficulties. Before we left the apartment, he complimented Scout's demeanor and behavior, saying, "She doesn't have an aggressive bone in her body." Once outside, we had walked only a few steps when Chris praised our "step off" from the curb into the cross-walk.

It was clear that Chris had great hopes for us, and by the time we reached the river he was encouraging me to give the leash a firm tug, pulling sharply from the waist, every time Scout got a little too far ahead. Henry tried the same technique, and we could both see that the chain collar was definitely helping. Scout seemed to understand what we were trying to teach her even before we returned to our apartment.

Back at home, Chris gave Henry and me a pep talk, encouraging us to continue with the slip collar and firm correction. Consistency and repetition would be our watchwords, and the use of the collar would remind Scout that we were serious about control-ling her.

Over the next few days, we were pleased to note that Chris's instruction had made a difference. Scout pulled less, and we began to trust her more. It helped that we had seen her walk perfectly and obediently, not only with Chris holding the leash but with me holding it. Now we knew she was capable of walking on the leash without misbehaving.

Even so, I could tell that Henry was brooding about the same issue I was. We were both having real trouble letting go of the positive approach; deep down, we still believed it would work. Besides, Scout's job was not to sniff out bombs. Her purpose in life was simply to get her exercise and be a great companion, to share our adventures, and to keep us moving.

Happily, we eventually came up with a method that worked for us and for Scout. By stopping dead in our tracks every time she pulled, we managed to significantly reduce the problem, even when she was wearing her regular collar. True, she still pulled hard when we approached the dog run, but she did that on the chain collar as well.

The slip collar took its place in the Scout drawer, along with the harness and Gentle Leader. All served as reminders that when yank came to pull, we could take any one of them out and temporarily keep Scout under stricter control. Sometimes Henry's back would ache after moving furniture, and he would use the slip collar. For my part, I would use it in bad weather, when the sidewalks and street were slick and dangerous.

In the end, the truth seemed to be that no single training approach consistently worked for us. We extracted the parts of Chris Velez's prescriptions that made the most sense to us and blended them with some of Diane Abbott's positive-training rules. We also decided that training was fundamentally an issue of trust: as Scout became an integral part of our lives, we needed to trust her, she needed to trust us, and—perhaps most important—we needed to trust ourselves to know how best to raise her.

~

As spring approached, I was eager to show Chris that Scout had made real progress. As it happened, I had been invited to a promotional event in Manhattan for Swiffer, a line of cleaning products that, among other things, does a good job of collecting dog hair. The event was a cocktail party, humans and dogs invited, at a midtown hotel, and the guest of honor was Cesar Millan, Swiffer's celebrity sponsor. Since I was hoping to interview Millan and I knew Chris admired him, I called Chris and invited him to join Henry, Scout, and me at the party.

The scene was charmingly chaotic. Scout was very excited to see Chris, as well as the dozen other dogs who were "guests" at the soiree. The party's reception area—which led out to the hotel's roof deck—was adorned with oversized martini glasses that had been placed on the floor. The glasses, which were about the size of large dog water bowls, were filled with home-baked dog biscuits in three different flavors.

Scout was indifferent to the celebrity in our midst, but once she discovered what those martini glasses contained and realized that their rims were level with her snout and mouth, she was in heaven. Every time I tried to lead her away from the biscuits, Scout pulled hard on her leash. Observing this struggle, Chris gently took the leash and led Scout away from the dog biscuits. She followed him happily toward the roof deck, where many of the other owners and dogs had already gathered.

Out on the deck was Millan himself, and I walked up to him. Wearing jeans and a diamond earring, he looked relaxed and very Californian. He was not surrounded by handlers, as many celebrities are, and I found him friendly and eager to talk.

Dog Whisperer, Millan's Friday night TV show on the National Geographic channel, is now in its seventh season and is still one of the most highly rated cable programs. At forty-one, Millan is an industry unto himself, with popular books and other commercial tie-ins to the show. For someone who was born in Mexico and spoke no English when he arrived in this country illegally twenty years ago, he has come far. Now a superstar dog trainer (and a U.S. citizen), he has helped such famous clients as Oprah Winfrey, Nicolas Cage, and Will Smith.

But at this point in his career, Millan is also a man under fire. A growing chorus of critics has assailed his vision of dog owners as assertive pack leaders and labeled his approach to training as too punitive. Some say his techniques—including the alpha roll, which involves forcing a dog to roll on its side—are dangerous and can be psychologically damaging to dogs. (Indeed, his show warns that viewers should not copy his techniques without consulting a professional.) Some respected animal behaviorists, like Temple Grandin, also claim that Millan misunderstands the behavior of wolves and how it applies to dogs.

I had read a lot of the criticism, including an oft-cited op-ed article in the *Times* called "Pack of Lies." And, of course, Diane Abbott had talked to me about why positive reinforcement trainers believe that Millan's pack-leader approach is completely wrong.

When reading Millan's latest book, *Cesar's Rules*, I was surprised to note that he goes out of his way to document his use of positive reinforcement "in one form or another" in two-thirds of his first 140 TV shows. And in defense of his leadership-focused techniques, he points out that his work is mostly with problem dogs. As he puts it in his book, "What I'm doing isn't dog 'training' but dog rehabilitation."

In the book, Millan also cites the influence of Dr. Ian Dunbar, the guru of lure-reward training. Millan tells the story of a session during which his pit bull Junior learned to respond to voice commands (Millan usually prefers to work in silence) and picked up an entirely new command—Down—in the course of a few minutes thanks to the use of rewards. Clearly, the Dog Whisperer is trying to send the message that he has an open mind about methodology. He is also trying to establish credibility with his critics without compromising the training principles that made his reputation.

As Millan and I chatted on the roof deck, I mentioned a number of the criticisms I'd heard about his methods. He didn't seem in any way defensive or offended. "I don't disagree with anyone disagreeing with me," he said. "All the people who disagree with me have never walked with a pack of dogs," he said. Back in California, Millan said he had sixteen pit bulls living at his training facility; even when off-leash, the dogs followed him obediently when he walked around his property. Millan had also trained rottweilers, another difficult breed known for aggression, to follow him without leashes. "Animals do not follow unstable pack leaders," he told me in his calm but assertive tone.

That comment bothered me, but not because I believed he was wrong. I thought about Scout's problem with pulling—maybe she dragged me this way and that because I was an unstable leader.

I described Scout's problem to Millan. His response was sympathetic but direct. "She loves you, but that doesn't mean she will follow you." Continuing, he said, "Too many people say, 'My dog is my baby, my dog is my soul mate.' But we need to honor that a dog is a dog."

These words made supreme sense to me. The setting for our conversation was more than a little surreal—I'd been to plenty of Manhattan cocktail parties, but never one quite like this—yet Millan was right. Dogs are not our soul mates. They are their own beings.

A moment later, Chris approached us with Scout, and Millan gave her an admiring pat. Then it was time for him to return to the reception area and demonstrate his training techniques to the crowd of thirty or so humans and their dogs.

The Swiffer people had arranged for a passel of six-week-old puppies to serve as Millan's trainees during the demonstration. When the puppies walked to the front of the room with Millan, Scout could not be contained, so Chris led her to the front row where she could see everything. Spotting her and seeing how much she yearned to be part of the performance, Millan invited Scout to join in, even though she was a lot bigger than the tiny pups. He drew our attention to the way the puppies eagerly sniffed Scout, thereby using their sense of smell to judge the newcomer in their midst.

Scout proudly strutted around the puppies and

Henry, Jill, Cesar Millan, Chris Velez, and Scout
at the Swiffer event *(Ken Taro)*

then bowed in front of one of them, inviting it to play. "That is what dogs should do," Millan told the audience. The audience clapped, and Scout seemed to bask in the attention. Then, her moment in the sun over, she followed Chris to the back of the room, where she resumed her hunt for biscuits.

CHAPTER NINE

It is simply breathtaking how much a puppy learns and changes in the first year. Sure, Scout still pulled, but as a full-grown girl she had also become the best kind of companion: empathetic when I'd had a bad day at work, funny and always ready to play, and a good-natured advocate for the beneficial effects of exercise. Now, as the cold weather at last receded and the first forsythia buds began to show themselves in Connecticut and Manhattan, Scout regularly persuaded me to crawl off the couch and go for a good walk.

So much of my experience of Scout's first twelve months reminded me of the years when I was surrounded by small children, a passage I missed more than I admitted to myself. When I walked into our apartment at night, Scout would invariably be waiting for me with a toy in her mouth—usually Louis the Lobster or Crazy Henrietta—and I would often think of my kids and how attached they were to their playthings. (I was pretty attached to them, too; in fact, Will once told me he suspected that I loved playing with his action figures more than he did.)

As happened with our children, Scout would sometimes appear at our bedside in the middle of the night or near dawn, lonely and needing our company. She would also occasionally bark or become agitated when she heard strange noises, particularly when she was new to Manhattan. And she was especially mischievous early in the morning. If we didn't give her enough attention after waking, she was liable to steal one of my socks or a glove and chew it to pieces. Or if Henry and I were making our bed, she was sure to pick that moment to jump on the bed and mess the covers. Like Cornelia and Will, Scout loved it when we covered her with our sheets and blankets.

But just as children can sometimes be infuriating, Scout's antics would occasionally drive me just short of crazy. One night I had to stay at the office unusually late, but since I knew that Henry was at home working on a report, I wasn't worried about leaving Scout alone. When I got back to our apartment, however, it was immediately apparent that Henry had failed to keep an eye on our devious pup. There was Henry, hunched over his computer and completely absorbed in his work—and there was Scout, snoozing in the front hall with the wreckage of my favorite cowboy boots nearby. A pair of brown Luccheses, they had been specially ordered from Texas and had turned a wonderful, warm color with age. The boots were one of the only pairs of good leather shoes I could comfortably wear after my unfortunate encounter with the truck; otherwise, my closet was filled with orthopedic flats. Clearly Scout had broken into my closet, stolen one of the boots, and gnawed off its burnished, pointed toe. She must have spent a good deal of time accomplishing this wicked task. Annoyed, I accused Henry of not paying enough attention. "I thought she was just chewing on her bone," Henry explained sheepishly. From that point on, we slid pens through the closet's door handle so Scout could no longer break in and steal my footwear.

As was also true when our kids were little, much of our social life now revolved around our friendships with people who shared our giddy fascination with the newest members of our families. When we got together with Marian and Howard and others like them, a lot of our talk revolved around our pups. (At least we didn't have to immerse ourselves in endless discussion about which grade school Scout could or should go to.) And when we encountered strangers on the street or in a park who also had dogs, we often struck up animated conversations about issues small and large that we inevitably had in common.

Scout, meanwhile, was growing up so quickly that we could barely keep pace with how much she was changing. She no longer feared German shepherds, and she was now relaxed and happy around her dog friends and confident when meeting unfamiliar dogs. She never once displayed a bit of aggression, even when strange dogs suddenly growled at her in Manhattan. She had now reached her adult weight of eighty pounds—twenty more than originally predicted!—but she was still in love with Charlie, the toy Havanese that lived across the street, and she was very careful not to trample him or step on his tiny paws during play. Charlie still invited Scout to chase him and roughhouse with him, and Scout continued to steal Charlie's toys and gobble the small rawhide bones that Charlie, with his Lilliputian teeth, would spend months chewing on.

Although Scout was now completely at ease in the city, her happiest times were still in Connecticut when she met her friends at the farm and romped in the fields without a leash. On the weekends, Scout and I frequently met up with my friend Barbara Pearce and her young Lab, Xena, who was extremely wild as a pup and remained so. Scout and Xena would tear around the farm at top speed, swim in the mucky ponds even when the water was freezing, and wrestle happily in the mud. After a playdate with Xena, Scout was always absurdly filthy. I would look at her dirty face and suddenly remember the look on my kids' faces after they'd spent a spring morning playing in the mud. Never have I seen a lovelier image of pure happiness.

That March, I spent an afternoon with Lee Gibson, who had recently received good news from Fidelco: Viggo had successfully completed his final course of training. Lee showed me several pictures of Viggo participating in his classes, which involved intensive work with professional trainers who acted out the roles of blind people. He looked happy and proud, and as Lee showed me the photos, she did too. Of the ten dogs in Viggo's litter, he was one of only three who ultimately passed.

Soon after that visit, I was honored when Lee invited

me to go with her to watch Viggo complete one of his final training walks. We drove to Hartford and met a director from Fidelco at a downtown street corner. The director instructed us to stand at the curb as Viggo passed by; she also told us not to distract Viggo or try to establish contact with him in any way. Viggo would be walking with the director of Fidelco's foster program and leading her as he would a blind person. He had been trained to walk around the many obstacles presented by a city sidewalk; he had also been taught to listen to the traffic so he would know when to cross the street.

Lee and I waited for a few minutes, and then suddenly there he was, walking beside a tall female trainer. Viggo wore a heavy harness, and he appeared thinner and older than when I had last seen him. He also looked so calm and responsible that it was nearly impossible to believe that this was the same dog that had once bullied our little pup.

Lee and I watched as Viggo carefully led the trainer around a tree that was almost directly in their path. Then, at the entrance to the old G. Fox department store, Viggo led the trainer through a revolving door, something I couldn't imagine Scout mastering. Only once, when they passed a group of pigeons, did the trainer have to correct Viggo. For a split second, he seemed about to lunge at the birds, but the trainer brought him immediately back into line. Scout, of course, would have ripped out my arm to get to the pigeons.

After the training walk, Lee was allowed to visit with Viggo for an hour. I gave her one of Scout's favorite balls to pass on to Viggo, but Lee was clearly anxious about having to say good-bye to him all over again. Still, we were both amazed to think that the hapless pup that she had begun working with a little more than a year ago was about to become an actual guide dog for the blind. The hundreds of hours that Lee had spent training and socializing Viggo had paid off.

As I drove home that day, I reminded myself that if Viggo could learn so much in a relatively short time, Scout too could eventually learn not to pull and even not to eat cowboy boots. But Henry and I would have to rededicate ourselves to training her, spend many more hours working with her, and give her plenty of attention and love along the way. In the coming months, we would undoubtedly see as much backsliding as progress; we would also, I was sure, experience surprises both bad and good. But if Chris Velez could train dogs to sniff bombs and Lee could train Viggo to work as a guide dog, we could do our part for Scout.

We would do it not because Scout would be working in the real world, but because we knew she wanted to learn how to master the job of being a very good dog.

As Scout approached her first birthday, Henry and I were eager to take her back to Thistledown and show her off to Donna Cutler, the breeder. We also wanted Scout to have a reunion with her mother, Tess, and the rest of her relatives. Partly we wanted to see if Scout shared any of her blood family's physical and personality characteristics, but we were also curious to learn whether, as we had read in some books, the mother-puppy bond remained strong even after separation.

We made the necessary arrangements with Donna, but when the day for the reunion came I was unable to go. Disappointed, I insisted that Henry bring back a full report, and when he returned from Thistledown he gave me a detailed description of the visit, which began when he once again followed instructions and carefully wiped his paws before entering Donna's house, with Scout right behind him.

Scout greeted Donna enthusiastically and eagerly accepted her admiring pats, but she did not seem to remember Donna. Henry and Scout followed Donna

Donna Cutler introducing Scout to her ancestors

outside to the wire-fenced dog pen, where more than half a dozen beautiful British goldens were lounging about. At the sight of Donna and Scout, they got to their feet, moved briskly to the gate, and gave off a mighty homecoming howl, making Scout feel wonderfully welcome. But would she know or get along with her relatives, especially her mother?

First Donna brought out Tess, Scout's gorgeous, one-eyed mother. They greeted each other the way two dog acquaintances would; there was no great joy, just a little sniff, and then Scout wanted to play. But Tess declined the invitation and soon displayed more interest in Donna than in her offspring. So much for the theory that female dogs remain attached to their pups!

Such a cool hello from a birth mother might have been devastating to a human, but mother dogs often become somewhat detached from their puppies after weaning. Interestingly, this may be an evolutionary response brought about by millennia of contact with humans, who usually take over the care of puppies when they're still quite young. (That's what a number of scientists suggest, anyway. Given that a new mother has as many as ten pups feeding off her day and night, I think Momma may just need a break!)

Next came Scout's grandmother, who Henry thought actually looked more like Scout than Tess did. The

Scout (left) with her ancestors

two dogs immediately took off and began running in circles, which delighted Scout. After a few minutes of play, out came great-grandmother, who greeted Scout with just a sniff or two. Then it was time for a group photograph of the maternal line going back four generations. Looking at this remarkable collection of beauties, Henry felt a little sad to think that Scout couldn't continue the line, but that was our choice, and Donna's rule, from the beginning.

Scout's father—a famous Austrian golden named Patrick—no longer lived with Donna; he had moved to New Hampshire. But to end the procession of relatives, Donna brought out Scout's grandfather, who was much larger than any of the females but still a calm fellow and very handsome to boot. As Henry took a few group photos, he and Donna agreed that it was this big guy whom Scout most resembled.

Once the dogs were put back in their pen, Donna remarked that she thought Scout's temperament was excellent. She also said that Scout could be a good candidate for advanced training, which might include retrieving ducks from the water. As it happened, Donna had kept the last of Scout's littermates, Johnnie, and he had become a field champion, winning blue ribbons in a competition in Canada. Donna showed Henry the two ducks she kept in her freezer for Johnnie's practice sessions, but in the end he politely declined her offer to allow Scout a little taste of the wild.

As for the physical conformation that set the benchmark for judging the shows in which Donna's dogs often competed, Donna said that Scout was a bit high in the back, and her feet were a little "eastie-westie," or too far turned out. Otherwise, Donna declared that her little Cindy Lou had grown up to be a very pretty girl. She was happy to hear that we had worked so hard to train her, and that we were using a clicker and mostly following the precepts of the positive method.

After saying good-bye to Donna, Henry packed Scout into the car. From what he could tell, this reunion with her blood family had meant no more to Scout than any other visit with a human who owned dogs. She slept most of the way back to our house in Connecticut, which is exactly what she had done during that first trip home as a new pup. But the road we had traveled since then was a lot longer than the 125 miles that separated Donna's house from ours.

—

Donna's expert assessment of Scout's appearance may have quashed any lingering thoughts about entering

Scout in high-powered competitions, but it didn't prevent us from entering her in an annual event in our Connecticut town called the Parade of Pooches. The show takes place on our town green and is a completely unofficial, just-for-fun competition. It only resembles the real Westminster show—held each year at Madison Square Garden and the pinnacle of U.S. dog shows—in that the dogs are judged by breed and given awards. And there is no Best in Show award, the crown jewel of Westminster and the title of the very funny Christopher Guest movie that spoofs the affair.

In February, I had attended the real Westminster Kennel Club Dog Show, which was established in 1877 and is the second-longest continuously held sporting event in the United States. Henry and I have always been fans of the show, which is broadcast on cable television each year. We especially love it when the handlers—who invariably dress in starchy British clothes—look like the dogs they are showing. In the past, we had often watched the show with Buddy wedged between us on our bed. This year, even though I had tickets, Henry preferred to watch the show with Scout from home, so I went with a friend.

To my eye, the show seemed pretty true to the movie (or perhaps vice versa), complete with stressed-out owners madly blow-drying their dog's fur in the so-called benching area off the floor where the judging rings were. To assist the reporters covering the show, the show's organizers provided hourly briefings on the dogs—more than 2,500 of them—who were the stars of the competition. Meanwhile, journalists were invited to sessions with representatives from all of the major pet supply and pet food companies, all of whom were frantically trying to attract media coverage for their latest products. (Pedigree, a major sponsor of the show, tried unsuccessfully to persuade me to attend a tutorial on its latest, supposedly healthier brand of dry food.)

As with most aspects of dog life, the Westminster show has become a combat zone. Not only are the owners fiercely competitive, but in recent years a conflict has broken out between the American Kennel Club—the primary registry of purebred dog pedigrees in the United States and a promoter of the show—and its numerous critics. These critics argue that by putting a premium on dogs' appearances, the AKC encourages unhealthy breeding techniques, such as mating two dogs with champion traits who are too closely related. The critics also claim that other characteristics—a dog's instinct for performing a specific sort of work, for instance—are not prized sufficiently. Recently some owners have gone so far as to boycott the AKC and the Westminster show.

I timed my visit to the show so that I could see the

Best in Breed judging of the golden retrievers. (All the competing goldens, of which there were several dozen, were the much deeper, honey color that is the classic standard for the breed.) My first stop was the benching area backstage, where giant poodles in hair curlers and other dogs of just about every breed primped for their moment in the ring. Next I moved up to the stands and took a seat near a number of the owners' families, some of whom had traveled from as far as California and had been competing in dog shows every weekend for the past year.

When it came time for the goldens to compete, I watched the dogs and their handlers with particular interest. The male and female dogs were judged separately, and all were put through their paces briskly and without a lot of obvious grandstanding. I couldn't help but notice that not a single one of the dogs pulled when their handlers strutted before the judges. Inevitably, perhaps, I tried to imagine Scout joining the goldens vying for a prize, but I got no farther than conjuring a vision of Scout wildly pulling me past the judges and right out of the Garden.

I enjoyed my visit to the Westminster show, and it made me look forward to our show in Connecticut.

Diane Abbott, who would serve as one of the judges, assured me that it was nothing like the extravaganza in New York; she also convinced me that Scout would enjoy it and that it was impossible to be disgraced. Diane told me that just about every dog won a ribbon, which put me in mind of those long-ago days when Cornelia and Will, like almost every other child, had come home at the end of the school year with some kind of trophy.

The morning of the show, Scout was excited by our vigorous brushing of her fur, and I even brushed her teeth for the occasion. As we approached our town's green, she began pulling with nearly all her strength when she saw the great number of dogs gathering there. And she was ecstatic when she saw Diane, who promptly gave her a dog biscuit from the registration table.

About a dozen other dogs had been entered in the golden retriever category, but Scout was the only platinum blonde. Scout was thrilled to be measured and assessed by the volunteer judges, and she gave her competitors a good sniff, as if to size them up. When one of the judges passed us, he looked at Scout and said, "Oh, she's a beauty." Helpless with pride, I beamed.

At the real Westminster show, dogs perform for the judges in four separate rings simultaneously.

Scout at the Parade of Pooches show

Here, the breeds are judged in sequence as they walk around our makeshift ring. This year, the goldens didn't get their chance until near the end, and soon Scout became restless, barking and pulling. Diane came over to distract her and play, and finally it was our turn to walk in a circle in front of the judges.

I led Scout on the walk. She proudly strutted as we moved around the ring—and to my amazement she didn't pull on her leash. I was absurdly grateful for this reprieve, and the experience brought back vivid memories of watching my children in school musical productions. Listening to them rehearse was often painful, but their performances, even when my heart was in my throat, were usually splendid.

When the results of the Best in Breed competition were announced, we were thrilled. When judged against her fellow goldens, Scout won a coveted blue ribbon for having "the longest ears"—a category, needless to say, that isn't included at the real Westminster show. I had never noticed that Scout's ears were longer than any other golden's, but we would take victory however it came. When the show was over, we packed Scout and her ribbon into the back of our car; when we got home, we looked for the ribbon but found only a few telltale bits of shiny blue thread. She had eaten it.

Scout's actual birthday was April 9. Henry and I agreed that there was no question about the appropriate venue for our celebration: the farm. Fortunately, the weather that day was perfect, still brisk but brilliantly sunny. In a few weeks, the gardeners would be back at the farm tending their bulbs, vegetables, and herbs, and we would have to make the garden areas off-limits again. But for now, Scout and her pals still had the run of the place.

We had told other Breakfast Club walkers about Scout's big day, and we also called Barbara Pearce and asked her to bring her Lab, Xena, who was almost exactly Scout's age. Henry, Scout, and I arrived a bit early, and Barbara pulled in a few minutes later. Scout got excited the moment she caught sight of Barbara's car, and when the car came to a stop I let her bound over to greet Xena. They immediately began wrestling and running after each other, and Barbara, Henry, and I laughed as we watched their joyous reunion. We took photographs, too, but Scout and Xena moved so quickly that it was almost impossible to get a decent picture.

Barbara and I marveled over how far both of our dogs had come since first meeting in Marian's backyard as tiny, teething pups. Less than a year ago, they

Scout, Xena, and the birthday cookie

were little bundles of fur falling over their own paws as they chased each other. And it was at Marian's that Scout had first experienced the pleasures of water when she splashed about in a plastic baby pool, one that was now far too small to hold her.

Soon Marian and Clyde arrived with Cyon and Bunny, Scout's truest and most constant companions. Scout was so busy chasing Xena that at first she barely took time out to say hello to her old friends. But I was pleasantly surprised when Scout and Xena responded to my call, stopped running around, and then sat obediently while waiting for me to share a treat with them. To mark Scout's birthday, I had purchased a yogurt-frosted, heart-shaped dog cookie from the local pet store. I split the cookie in half, and in no time the two dogs wolfed it down.

A few minutes later, Lee Gibson pulled into the farm's parking lot. I was eager for Lee to join Scout's birthday celebration because she had been so helpful with Scout's training.

As Lee approached us, I saw something moving at her heel. For a second I thought a rabbit was walking next to her, but then I realized that it was actually a brand-new puppy. It was another German shepherd, but he was so young that he was all ears and paws. Lee told us that his name was Caleb, and that this one was hers to keep.

Caleb the puppy

As I gave Lee a hug and said hello, I saw that she had circles under her eyes. I also noticed that she was a bit wary when Scout and Xena, now such big girls, raced over to sniff Caleb and check out the new kid on the block. This was me a year ago, bone-tired and worrying over every new experience that came Scout's way.

Now, as Scout approached Caleb, she made a gentle bow, her front paws sticking out in front of her. It was a dog's invitation to play, a universal gesture that is performed countless times each day all over the world. And as Caleb accepted the invitation and cavorted with Scout, the cycle began anew.

EPILOGUE

When I turned fifty, my friend Jane Mayer gave me the perfect gift. Jane works for the *New Yorker*, and in the magazine's archives she found a photograph of one of my favorite writers, E. B. White, taken at his classic Maine farmhouse. White, then almost eighty, was cradling Susy, his beloved Westie, one of the last in a long line of devoted canine companions. Buddy was still very much alive when I received that photo, and it delighted me to know that the Westie breed connected me to the author of *Charlotte's Web* and some of journalism's finest essays. In one of those essays, in fact, White dispensed the wisest comment about raising a puppy I have ever come across: "A really companionable and indispensable dog is an accident of nature. You can't get it by breeding for it, and you can't buy it with money. It just happens along."

When Scout came into my life, an indispensable dog did just happen along. It wasn't the clickers or puppy kindergarten or feeding her the right meals that made her such a fine companion. More than anything else, it was the passage of time, and the inevitable calming process that occurred as Scout aged. Almost as important was the change in Henry and me: we came to understand that everything we do is more fun and interesting when Scout is by our side.

Whether contentedly snoozing while we watch UConn's basketball team snatch a victory from Arizona, or sniffing at some daffodils as they poke out of the hard winter soil near the Hudson River, Scout has become essential to our daily lives. Moreover, what we choose to do with an hour or an afternoon often mirrors what she most enjoys. When she wants to engage in a game of chase or keep-away or go for a brisk walk, so do we. And no matter what we do, Scout's fundamental sweetness and exuberance make the experience joyful. She is almost always in a state of delight, unlike so much of the world that I help capture each day for readers of the *New York Times*.

Which is not to say that Scout doesn't have an occasional bad moment or misbehave. Every once in a while, for instance, her face will appear above the table line with a hopeful expression. And she still pulls on her leash, though not as savagely. But she has long since conquered her fear of German shepherds, and not long ago she picked Caleb as her favorite walking companion. The happy accidents of nature continue.

Looking back on our first year with Scout, I am amazed by how quickly it passed. The experience of bringing this whirlwind of untamed energy into our lives was so intense and involving that I sometimes felt as if the puppy months would kill us. Like most owners, we worried about everything, from Scout's constant chewing to her fussy eating to her sudden illness. Then, in the blink of an eye, she was fully grown and fully attached to us. And just as our love for her grew to be almost boundless, she became unfailingly loyal and perceptive about our needs and desires.

This almost ineffable transference fascinated me from the start, and it was the main reason I decided to chronicle Scout's first year. I knew that Henry and I enjoyed nearly ideal circumstances, with the time, space, and means to dote on a dog. But as one half of a two-career couple in late middle age, I also knew that some of the stresses we were feeling as new puppy owners were universal, as was the humor inherent in the experience. After all, no matter who you are or what you do for a living, it is invariably humbling to try to persuade a puppy to do your bidding.

Even before Scout arrived, I thought it might be fun to share some of my experiences and draw on the response of the *Times*'s readers. I did so by writing a series of columns for the newspaper's Web site. My hope was that those who followed the column would become engaged by our imperfect efforts to raise a puppy and offer copious advice, which they did. I also asked readers to send in photos of their own pups, an invitation that attracted such an avalanche of snapshots that at one point the paper's Web site crashed.

Because I have dedicated much of my career in journalism to editing and writing serious investigative stories, some of my readers—and a few of my friends as well—found it strange that I was publicly sharing my nervousness over Scout's first day of puppy kindergarten or my persistent sadness over the loss of Buddy. But as I continued writing the column and providing updates on Scout's adventures, I found a natural story emerging, one that connected me to plenty of other *Times* readers who, like me, were simply crazy about their dogs.

⁓

Almost from the beginning, Scout seemed to accept that my demanding job meant she would rarely receive my undivided attention. She learned, for instance, that although weekend mornings were an apparently languid time, they were in fact dedicated to a longer and even closer reading of the *Times*, page by page and section by section. Though this ritual required that she wait until later than usual to go to the farm or the dog run, she was never impatient. Reflecting on this one day, I realized that Scout didn't need me to spend all my time focused on her. Instead, what she most wanted was my unwavering love.

This, I came to understand, was my test. During her first year with us, Scout had passed *her* test: she had learned how to be a good dog and become a loving companion. But as her second year with us began, I was keeping a guilty secret, which was that sometimes I still longed for Buddy. The essential question remained: could I ever give my whole heart to Scout?

A first, partial answer came in the summer of 2010. More than three years had passed since my terrible accident in Times Square, and I had almost fully recovered from my injuries. I felt so confident that I could meet just about any physical challenge—or at least any challenge appropriate for a woman my age— that I decided to take a break from Scout and accompany Henry and his sister, Elisabeth, on a trip to Yellowstone National Park. Elisabeth loved to hike, and I persuaded her to tackle some fairly demanding trails with Henry, a guide, and me.

We enjoyed three days of excellent hiking, but on the last day of our visit, Henry was suffering from altitude sickness and so decided to take it easy. Still game, Elisabeth and I got our guide, Jeff, to take us on a climb to Specimen Ridge, one of the most scenic places in the park. The hike was about seven miles up and back, which would be difficult but not beyond my capacity—or so I thought.

Jeff was a bit worried that we might come across one or more bears, especially since two people had died earlier in the summer after a horrifying encounter with grizzlies. He reassured us by bringing along some bear spray, and the climb up the ridge proved to be no problem. Near the top, we passed a stunningly beautiful family of elks, and when we reached the summit I lay flat on the ground and looked up at the sun. "I can die happy now," I said to Jeff.

Famous last words. About halfway down the mountain, I slipped on scree and tumbled a hundred feet down a steep slope. My head must have hit something in the fall, and I was knocked unconscious. Elisabeth, with bear spray in hand, slid down to me while Jeff ran for help, which arrived in about twenty-five minutes. By then I was conscious, but my face was a mass of cuts and bruises, my left arm was broken in two places, and one of my vertebrae was cracked. I had to be airlifted to a hospital in Bozeman, Montana, where surgeons, once again, reassembled my bones with titanium.

I felt like a total idiot, although my doctors assured me that such falls are fairly common in the park. When they finally cleared me to fly back to New York, Henry and I both worried that our exuberant puppy would jump on me and reinjure my arm and back. But we had both missed Scout terribly on our longer-than-expected trip, and I couldn't wait to see her, whatever the risk.

When Henry opened our front door, Scout didn't bound over to us. She didn't even have a toy in her mouth. Happily and calmly, she came to greet us and then waited for Henry and me to hug and pat her. When I sat down on our living room couch, she immediately lay at my feet. She stayed there for hours and got up only to follow me to the kitchen or bathroom.

For the next week, that was our routine. I was the

patient on pain medication, but Scout behaved as if she were on Valium. She was curious about the brace and bandage on my arm, but she never even jostled me. Other than going for walks with Henry, Cornelia, or Will, she spent all her energy protecting and guarding me. Whenever I set myself up on the couch, she would lie down a couple of feet away. When I moved to our bedroom, she would take up a position at the foot of the bed.

During my convalescence, Scout's breathing and the sight of her white back rising and falling made me feel cozy and safe. About ten days after returning home, I was at last well enough to take her out for a walk. This time, there was absolutely no pulling. Scout seemed to know that I needed her to behave, and she rose to the occasion valiantly. I have no doubt that I recovered from these new injuries more quickly because of her.

I had never felt closer to Scout than after my accident in Yellowstone, and that remained true throughout the fall. I won't say that I stopped thinking about Buddy altogether, but Scout proved to be such a loving and generous companion that my attachment to her grew even stronger.

That Christmas we were buried in snow, as one of the hardest winters in history descended on New York and Connecticut. Then Henry left for California on a business trip, leaving Scout and me alone in our apartment. Within a day or two, we developed a bad case of cabin fever and so decided to go on an extended walk.

It was a freezing Sunday—the temperature was below ten degrees—but at least the sun was shining. Since the funky dog run was iced over and grimy, I didn't want to begin our walk by taking Scout there. Instead, I attached her leash and we began walking uptown.

One of Buddy's favorite places in New York City was Washington Square Park, with its famous archway and two dog runs, one reserved for small dogs weighing less than twenty-five pounds and another for larger breeds. At twenty-two pounds, Buddy was the big man on campus in the park's small run, and he loved strutting around the place as if he owned it. But the park was about a mile and a half from our loft, so taking Buddy there required extra time and energy. In fact, when we visited the park near the end of his life, I often had to carry Buddy part of the way home because he was dragging and wheezing so badly.

For some reason—actually, I knew the reason all too well—I hadn't been back to the Washington

Square dog runs since Buddy's death almost four years earlier. But now, on this bitterly cold afternoon, it seemed like just the right moment to go. Though Scout certainly wouldn't be allowed in the small dog run, I thought she might enjoy the larger area.

The trip north through the wintry city was lovely. Several people stopped to admire Scout, including a little girl who asked if she could pet her. "She's so bee—u—tiful," the little girl chimed. But as we approached Washington Square and then passed by the small dog run, I couldn't help but feel melancholy.

Scout entered the big dog run warily. A yellow Lab came over and gave her a halfhearted sniff before moving on to play with other friends. A pack of hounds chased one another, and Scout watched them enviously. Most of the dogs seemed to know each other well and none showed much interest in her. As Scout padded around in the snow and tried to make friends, I sat on a bench and felt sad for her.

Before long, though, a bundled-up man in a black down parka entered the dog run with a white golden retriever that looked like Scout's identical twin. This dog—named Daisy, as I quickly learned—bounded right over to Scout, who immediately went into her bow position. In an instant, the two were off, jumping up toward each other, wrestling and chasing. Like Scout, Daisy was about a year and a half old. She had been born in Canada and now weighed seventy-five pounds.

Daisy's owner, a gregarious fellow named Jeff, introduced himself and sat down to share my bench. For the next half hour, while the two dogs made friends, Jeff and I had an animated conversation about the remarkable qualities of English golden retrievers. "They really love playing with their own kind," Jeff observed. Before Daisy, he had had two other goldens. The last one had lived to fourteen, a ripe old age for a large, sporting breed. When I told Jeff that we had had a terrier before Scout, he responded, "Well, now you know just how wonderful goldens are."

And I did. I also knew that Henry and I could not have asked for a friendlier, more loving, or more enthusiastic dog. To complete our voyage through the perils of late middle age, we needed a dog exactly like Scout. No, not a dog *like* her—we needed Scout and only Scout. Sitting in Washington Square Park with freezing toes on one of the coldest afternoons of the year, I suddenly felt warmer than I had in weeks. I had not forgotten Buddy, but he was now the dog that had been my ideal companion for a different, earlier time. Watching Scout play in the snow with her seeming twin, I knew that I had finally passed *my* test: I had completely given my heart to her.

It was time to turn toward home. I had a happy,

tired dog, and at the moment I couldn't imagine feeling any more fortunate. Once again I thought of E. B. White, who was not only a superb writer but a truly wise man. He understood that dogs made his life better, and he acknowledged their gift whenever he wrote about the smart collie of his youth, the eccentric dachshunds that meant so much to him during his middle years, and Susy the Westie, who kept him company when he was old and living alone. Even after reaching an age when he knew the next pup he purchased would probably outlive him, there he was with a dog in his arms. I hoped this would be true of my life, too, from irascible Buddy to vulnerable Dinah to loopy Scout—and, perhaps, to the puppies that would come after.

SELECTED BIBLIOGRAPHY

The books listed below, many of which are mentioned in the text, will help puppy owners gain insights into their pets. Collectively they offer a survival guide for the first year.

DOGS (GENERAL)

Elder, Janet. *Huck: The Remarkable True Story of How One Lost Puppy Taught a Family—and a Whole Town—About Hope and Happy Endings*. New York: Broadway Books, 2010. A touching story about how the human-canine bonds deepen when a dog is suddenly lost.

Morris, Willie. *My Dog Skip*. New York: Vintage, 1996. The classic coming-of-age story of a boy and his dog in the

South. Skip learns amazing tricks, including how to fetch and pay for bologna at the local store.

Quindlen, Anna. *Good Dog. Stay.* New York: Random House, 2007. The end-of-life experiences of Beau—Quindlen's Labrador retriever—offer lessons, humorous and sad, about a painful time for all dogs and their humans.

White, E. B. *Essays of E. B. White.* New York: First Perennial Classics, 1999. The wonderful wisdom of Fred, E. B. White's dachshund, animates some of the best essays written by the author of *Charlotte's Web.*

DOG AND ANIMAL BEHAVIOR

Bekoff, Marc. *Animals at Play: Rules of the Game.* Philadelphia: Temple University Press, 2008. Play is how animals learn the importance of truth and justice, as well as just about everything in the realm of social behavior.

Grandin, Temple, and Catherine Johnson. *Animals Make Us Human: Creating the Best Life for Animals.* New York: Mariner Books, 2010. The animal scientist and autism advocate offers unique insights into how dogs feel.

Horowitz, Alexandra. *Inside of a Dog: What Dogs See, Smell, and Know.* New York: Simon & Schuster, 2010. A psychologist with a Ph.D. in cognitive science, Horowitz tells what the world is like from a dog's point of view.

Thomas, Elizabeth Marshall. *The Hidden Life of Dogs.* London: Phoenix, 2003. An anthropologist with a gift for storytelling, Thomas describes the pack dynamic through her observations of the roamings of her dogs.

DOG TRAINING

Dunbar, Ian. *After You Get Your Puppy: . . . The Clock is Ticking.* Berkeley, CA: James & Kenneth Publishers, 2001. Dr. Dunbar is a veterinarian who helped popularize lure-reward-based training. This is one of several books he has written about his training method.

Millan, Cesar, and Melissa Jo Peltier. *Cesar's Rules: Your Way to Train a Well-Behaved Dog.* London: Hodder & Stoughton, 2011. The Dog Whisperer of television fame has been criticized by some for using overly disciplinary training methods, but this recent book is careful to include some material about positive, reward-based training.

The Monks of New Skete. *The Art of Raising a Puppy.* London: Little, Brown, 2011. The best commonsense guide to how a day with a puppy ought to unfold.

Pryor, Karen. *Don't Shoot the Dog!: The New Art of Teaching and Training.* Gloucestershire, England: Ringpress Books Ltd, 2002. The queen of clicker training explains her system.

Rugaas, Turid. *My Dog Pulls: What Do I Do?* Wenatchee, WA: Dogwise Publishing, 2005. A detailed, pictorial guide that should help owners and dogs break a bad habit.

Stilwell, Victoria. *It's Me or the Dog: How to Have the Perfect*

Pet. London: Collins, 2005. The positive training techniques embraced by the popular television dog expert.

DOG FOOD

Hotchner, Tracie. *The Dog Bible: Everything Your Dog Wants You to Know*. New York: Gotham Books, 2005. This volume, which offers basic information on a wide variety of dog issues, has lots of information about what dogs like to eat and why.

Nestle, Marion. *Pet Food Politics: The Chihuahua in the Coal Mine*. Berkeley: University of California Press, 2008. Written in the wake of a pet food contamination scandal, this is an authoritative look inside the multibillion-dollar pet food industry.

———, and Malden C. Nesheiml. *Feed Your Pet Right: The Authoritative Guide to Feeding Your Dog and Cat*. New York: Free Press, 2010. Credible information in this book will help you be smarter about the labeling and contents of dog food.

Photograph courtesy of *The New York Times*

JILL ABRAMSON, a best-selling and award-winning author, is the executive editor of *The New York Times*. An unabashed dog-lover, she has long been fascinated by the complex relationship between dogs and their owners. She, her husband, and Scout live in New York City and Connecticut.

TWO ROADS

stories ... voices ... places ... lives

Two Roads is the home of fabulous storytelling and reader enjoyment. We publish stories from the heart, told in strong voices about lives lived. Two Roads books come from everywhere and take you into other worlds.

We hope you enjoyed *The Puppy Diaries*. If you'd like to know more about this book or any other title on our list, please go to www.tworoadsbooks.com or scan this code with your smartphone to go straight to our site:

For news on forthcoming Two Roads titles, please sign up for our newsletter.

We'd love to hear from you.

enquiries@tworoadsbooks.com Twitter (@tworoadsbooks).